Education in the 80's:

HEALTH EDUCATION

The Advisory Panel

Martha D. Adams, Coordinator of Health Services, Birmingham Board of Education, Alabama

Deborah C. Bacon, School Nurse, Dallas, Texas

Betty S. Baker, Professor, Southeastern Louisiana University, Hammond

Loren B. Bensley, Jr., Professor of Health Education, Central Michigan University, Mount Pleasant

Helen P. Cleary, Associate Professor, Department of Family and Community Medicine, University of Massachusetts Medical School, Worcester

Edia J. Harris, Section Chief, School Nurse Program, Louisiana State Department of Education, Baton Rouge

Leona J. Haverkamp, School Nurse Practitioner, Cedar Rapids Community Schools, Iowa

Ann E. Nolte, Professor, Health Education, Illinois State University, Normal

Larry K. Olsen, Associate Professor and Chair, Health Science, Department of Health and Physical Education, Arizona State University, Tempe

Peggy F. Rufner, Coordinator of Health Services, Kettering City Schools, Ohio

Marian K. Solleder, Professor of Health Education and Coordinator of the Graduate Division, School of Health, Physical Education and Recreation, University of North Carolina at Greensboro

Education in the 80's:

HEALTH EDUCATION

Robert D. Russell
Editor
Southern Illinois University
at Carbondale

Classroom Teacher Consultant
Frances S. Hoffman
Seminole Senior High School
Florida

National Education Association
Washington, D.C.

Stock No. 3153–9–00 (paper)
3154–7–00 (cloth)

Note

The opinions expressed in this publication should not be construed as representing the policy or position of the National Education Association. Materials
published as part of the NEA Education in the 80's series are intended to be
discussion documents for teachers who are concerned with specialized interests
of the profession.

Library of Congress Cataloging in Publication Data
Main entry under title:

Education in the 80's—health education.

  (Education in the 80's)
  Bibliography: p.
  1. Health education. I. Russell, Robert D., 1926– II. Hoffmann, Frances S.
III. Series.
[DNLM: 1. Health education—Trends.   2. Forecasting WA18 H4334]
RA440.E38   613'.07   80–15821
ISBN 0–8106–3154–7
ISBN 0–8106–3153–9 (pbk.)

Contents

Editor

Robert D. Russell is Professor of Health Education at Southern Illinois University, Carbondale. He is the author of NEA/AMA's *Health Education,* of *The Last Bell Is Ringing,* and co-author of *Coping with Death and Dying.*

Classroom Teacher Consultant

Frances S. Hoffmann is a high school health education teacher in Seminole, Florida.

There seems to be a growing appreciation in America of the paramount importance of buoyant personal health. This new awareness is evident in many ways; one is the increasing enrollment in health education courses, and the earnestness generally displayed by the participating students. If health teachers are to affect the lives of students for the better in the decade ahead, they must impress upon them the fact that early in life they face *crucial* personal health decisions that, perhaps even more than subsequent professional health care, will largely determine their lifelong plane of personal vigor, opportunity, achievement, and even joy.

There is no dearth of reliable health information today. Indeed, the challenge is to find time to screen the mass of material available for course planning. Since health education has so many facets, and the time available in a semester is never adequate for fully covering so extensive a subject, the health educator must select fundamentals from the most important areas to supply students with "nuggets" to remember and benefit from in the years ahead. A resource book in which an eminent health educator presents the expertise of leaders in twelve major health-related areas is a most welcome research and preparation tool.

Education in the 80's: Health Education is truly a forward-looking *idea* book filled with practical, directly relatable guidance for the classroom teacher. It offers light in some important dark areas of our experience. It is an *exciting* book, and its excitement breeds enthusiasm and encouragement.

Robert D. Russell's model for positive *Holistic Health* in chapter 1 is an innovative and stimulating prospect for use in the classroom. His "wellsprings" of health will help students see more clearly the important relationships of the various aspects of health to their total well-being. The six wellsprings could be used to show these interrelationships at the beginning of the health course, or they could be given as handouts to small groups to encourage research or discussion of their importance. His positive holistic approach to health education will give teachers more confidence in teaching health as the total composite of body, mind, and spirit.

Daniel A. Girdano's chapter, *A Holistic Approach to Stress Reduction,* is a thought-provoking treatment of a problem that is very real in the lives of students. It will assist the teacher of the 80's in encouraging students to think of themselves as part of their environment, rather than considering their natural surroundings as something simply to be used. His ideas on teaching stress management lend themselves very effectively to small group discussions; or they may be the basis for short-term personal observation charts for analyzing individual behavior and lifestyles. Encouraging students to look at the things they do, and at the manner in which they may modify personal actions for the better, will give them greater confidence to take command of their lives and reduce the stresses to which they subject themselves. Girdano presents techniques that will enable health teachers to assist students to become better prepared physically and emotionally to withstand excessive stress, and to use the byproducts of stress arousal constructively.

Marigold A. Edwards's discussion of stress management strategies to reduce stress, to improve student self-concepts, and to expand learning potential is exciting. She indicates that the health educator might be the activator in a school to arouse interest in stress management training. If techniques such as those Edwards discusses could be taught to staff and students to enable them to successfully reduce unnecessary stress in their lives, the implications for the future would be staggering.

Betty W. Tevis emphasizes the importance of informing and encouraging young people through education to adopt beneficial lifestyles that reject injurious smoking, incorporate a nutritious well-balanced diet, and allow time to develop good cardiovascular health. Tevis encourages health educators to include antismoking education and emergency cardiac care as well as cardiopulmonary resuscitation in their programs. She also urges beginning heart health education as early as possible to reduce the very high incidence of heart-related diseases in this country. Prevention truly *is* the key.

As consumers, students must be able to select health-related products intelligently, distinguishing between beneficial products and practices, and promoted "quackery." They also need to discuss when they may safely care for minor ailments themselves, and when a physician is required. Charles R. Carroll and Warren E. Schaller give the health educator much-needed information and ideas for teaching these skills, in addition to providing new information on unconventional medicine such as faith healing and acupuncture.

A mind-expanding chapter by Adogbeji Lucky Oghojafor of the World Health Organization on nonscientific healing affords an interesting look at the medicine and health practices of foreign countries. It gives a rare insight into the health views and values of other cultures.

Nancy Lee Jose offers new thoughts on stereotyping in ageism and sexism. If health teachers are to have an impact in the 80's, they must strive to reduce these prejudices and stereotypes that we have all inherited. *Health Education in the 80's* also includes valued guidance for those teaching human sexuality in the public schools. Stephen J. Bender stresses the qualities for the teacher of the subject, and suggests a fourteen-point curriculum outline. This chapter alone should make the book a valued resource in the library of every health educator.

Robert D. Russell's chapter on teaching about alcohol, tobacco, and marijuana is provocative; and Geraldine Rockett emphasizes that drug education must be designed to help students make responsible decisions about any drug use, whether ethical, proprietary, legal, or illegal.

The chapter on death education by Kathleen Hoyt Middleton contains excellent teaching strategies relating to this previously neglected experience of all humankind.

The implications of health on an international scale, which are deeply involved in world politics, are explored by Marian V. Hamburg. This is an aspect not included in most health texts. The consideration of global problems, consequences, and possibilities thus enables the health teacher to introduce an added dimension to the health curriculum.

Finally, Gus T. Dalis and Ben B. Strasser discuss new thinking for the teaching of values development in health education that will be of interest to all concerned.

Education in the 80's: Health Education looks *forward;* it offers a highly informed appraisal of health education teaching requirements and opportunities in what will most certainly prove to be a period of tremendous change. More than any preceding decade, the 80's will be a time when teachers will be encouraged to "teach it like it is" in some heretofore ignored, marginally treated, and little understood subject areas. This book encourages our imagination, rekindles our enthusiasm, and restates the importance of attractively presented, unequivocal, health-related doctrine in the lives of the nation's youth. The editor and contributing authors deserve our gratitude—they have written for considerably more than the decade immediately ahead.

Frances S. Hoffmann
Health education teacher
Seminole Senior High School
Seminole, Florida

This is a book with a focus on the near future—1980 to 1989. We writers assume that our field, health education, will persist, maintain—yes, even flourish—in this decade. We are writing from the present. Some of us have—even cherish—a solid sense of our historical past. We know what health education has been, some from scholarship and some from experience. On the other hand, some of us know and care little about the past. We know what the present is, and that is sufficient for our attentions.

We all have the task of making some predictions about the state and direction of certain parts of health education in the 1980's—a difficult task. Nearly twenty years ago in *Medical Utopias,* Rene Dubos reminded us that

> Science provides methods of control for the problems inherited from past generations, but it cannot prepare solutions for the specific problems of tomorrow because it does not know what these problems will be. Physicians and public health officials, like soldiers, are always equipped to fight the last war.

Health educators, too, perhaps?

Who has the skill, the vision, and the right to "prophesy"? NEA must have used some process to decide that I was a proper predictor. I utilized some equally secret procedure to assemble this panel of health educators to write about health education in relation to the heart, the consumer, alcohol, sexuality—and the other topics exhibited in the Contents.

You'll see, however, that really unique, "far-out" predictions are rather rare. Instead, most of the writers tell of what they are doing and developing at present and then predict that more of the field will follow this lead on into the next decade. Other writers from the profession might tell other stories and see the future somewhat differently. This book is offered therefore more as a stimulus to thought than as a guaranteed glimpse of the 80's. It is, at least, a composite description of *a* future.

The writers are of both sexes and reside and educate in different parts of the United States (with one from Nigeria and one originally from New Zealand). Unfortunately for the concept of balance and relevance for the schools, with the exception of the Classroom Teacher Consultant for the manuscript, none of the writers is now a practicing public school teacher. Until 1979, Middleton was a junior high teacher in California. But the reality was that, understandably, I was not able to entice any functioning classroom teachers into writing with such a short deadline. My apologies.

Four authors are working in the areas they write about. Girdano is the codirector of an institute in the Colorado Rockies designed to help people function more positively personally and professionally. Tevis helps design and implement the programs she describes for the American Heart Association. Dalis and Strasser spend much of their professional time directing workshops for teachers in Los Angeles County, helping them deal more effectively with values.

Oghojafor is presently awaiting assignment by the World Health Organization to his home country, Nigeria, to implement there the basic premises he professes here. Rockett is associate director of the counseling center at a small eastern college. Middleton left her junior high kids to revise national health curricula for the School Health Education Project, part of the National Center for Health Education.

The rest of us struggle with the opportunities for teaching, research, writing, and service to the profession that are part of the university professor's life, in locations from California to New York, from Kentucky to Pennsylvania, and including voices from the Illinois and Indiana heartlands.

And, now, some comments on specific contributions. "A Holistic Approach to Stress Reduction" by Girdano received considerable comment from reviewers. It is important to iterate, therefore, that chapter 2 is a personal, philosophical perspective by the author, not a chapter based on research into other colleagues' approaches to stress management. It is a prime example of an offering designed to stimulate thinking —even controversy. It is not intended as the summary for the whole field, but as the observations and convictions of a recognized health educator who now is "doing his trip" full-time.

The manuscript submitted by Edwards, which became chapter 3, "Stress Management Education," was considerably longer, with both an extensive philosophical base and physiological data. The decision was made that the original version would have been too repetitive of chapter 2 and would have given more space to a particular area than it deserved. Therefore the next decision was to present the unique material from

Edwards on educational approaches. The research reporting therein will not satisfy strict academicians, but it is suggestive of present attempts to evaluate education in this area. The two chapters are thus intended to complement each other. Neither, by its style, is intended to encourage stress in you readers.

Chapter 4, "Heart Health Education," is offered as a description of education toward present and future prevention of a major health problem affecting Americans. It is also intended as an example of how voluntary agencies are cooperating with schools for better health education. It is not meant to say or infer that the Heart Association is the only agency so involved. The page limitation just made complete, specific coverage a mighty challenge.

Chapter 6, Oghojafor's contribution entitled "Nonscientific Healing: What Is No Longer Quackery?" is probably the most controversial. The intent is not to put down or disparage orthodox medicine. Still, it contains the message that medicine is not always effective, while other treatments may be. The call is for traditional healing and scientific medicine to cooperate with and learn from each other—for the benefit of patients. This could be more of a challenge than some members of the scientific community can accept.

Chapter 7, Jose's "Sexism and Ageism," is not exactly a balanced, cautious view of health education's largely unconscious preference for the male and the young, over females and the elderly. But Jose's zeal is reasonably moderate. Again, we need to consider this view (which actually comes out quite reasonably), as well as others that may be different from it.

Chapter 9 focuses on "Alcohol, Marijuana, and Tobacco," the drugs used most commonly by today's young people—and most likely to be used in the future. The coverage is not evenly divided because the major emphasis is on alcohol, with less space given to tobacco, and only some token pertinent remarks about "pot." However, some of Rockett's chapter 10, "Drug Education," also applies to marijuana, as an illegal drug.

There has been no indication that the chapters not mentioned need additional comment.

And so, dear reader, settle back for some variety of observations on where we in health education have been, are now, and shall be in the imminent future.

Robert D. Russell, Editor
Southern Illinois University
at Carbondale

CHAPTER 1

Holistic Health
Robert D. Russell

DIMENSIONS OF HEALTH

Health is a positive quality. Yes, that notion has been in our literature for many a year, but in the late 70's it came more alive. This leads to the first prediction for the 1980's: Health education will become ever more *positive* in its orientation.

What does this mean? Well, it suggests that the content for the field—the messages in textbooks—will focus more on the positive. In discussions of exercise, for example, there will be more words about varieties of exercise that benefit the total being and about how they can be worked into different lifestyles; there will be shorter discussions of the symptoms of poor physical fitness and of all the dangers in exercising.

As another example, nutrition will perhaps be broadened to the more functional "food selection and eating patterns." The thrust will be to have learners see different ways of balancing food intake with needs, with emphasis on the many combinations of useful foods. Fewer minutes will go to obesity, to nutritional deficiencies, and to the dangers in the eating scene. In the mental health area the key concept will shift from stress reduction to something like mental/emotional balance, with emphasis on various ways in which people can succeed, learn, and feel good about themselves.

Although there will continue to be a working relationship between the curative-rehabilitative medical fields and health education, there will be more emphasis on a positive, holistic health model and less dependence on the medical model. This means less talk about health matters as problems to solve and more consideration of them as complex relationships to understand and work with. Although "changing behavior" will still be a legitimate goal of some health education, there will be much more emphasis on reinforcing behavior and practices that are useful and health-enhancing.

Holistic

But holistic—what is health in a holistic view? It is the quality of functioning of the complete, total person in his/her particular environment or ecosystem. In the immediate post-World War II era, the World Health Organization presented us with a definition of health that clearly broadened the field. "Physical, mental, and social well-being" became the often-quoted boost toward a holistic view—a departure from the earlier definition, which was "merely the absence of disease or infirmity."

Over these 30 years or more, analysis has indicated a need to see "mental well-being" representing both the intellectual and the emotional, which, though interacting, may not be consistent with each other. For many years health educators have learned that objectives for increasing knowledge and for affecting attitudes may be quite different. In the 60's, for instance, the "cognitive domain" was considered different from the "affective domain." The holistic perspective now sees both areas as distinct but interacting dimensions of each individual. One possible term to describe this interplay of the rational and the emotive holistically is "mental/emotional balance."

Spiritual

The major addition, however, to considerations of wholeness in health is the *spiritual* dimension. Its underlying premise is that the human being is more than just body and mind—there is a human spirit that is more than the mental, emotional, and social; and there are ways in which people function spiritually.

Now it must be said immediately that the spiritual is an interesting and "different" dimension because some people are going to deny its existence—a few rather vociferously. It may help to understand this if we recall that as medicine developed scientifically, it acquired a naturalistic orientation because it was perceived that science could consider only the "natural world." An applicable perspective would be "Everything that exists, exists in quantity. Anything that exists in quantity can be measured." The unfortunate conclusion was "Anything that cannot be measured does not exist."

At any rate, the choice that medicine should be naturalistic-scientific *only* was a philosophical one. As a result health was seen in the same way; consequently, health education was not encouraged to consider the spiritual as a dimension or the soul as a reality.

Now this discussion began with the comment that the spiritual is a "different" sort of dimension; for while a few deny its reality, others accept it, yet view it in a variety of ways. Some are satisfied with the concept of a spirit within each person and therefore prize the interactions of spirits within people, evidenced by love, respect, honor, sacrifice. Some acknowledge and respect a power greater than themselves, evidenced in the nature and workings of the world. Finally, many believe in a God who relates to them personally, who can take action which influences, even determines, the way their lives go.

People of like beliefs tend to join together in religions and churches, supporting and being supported in their faith and practice. For some groups, notably Christian Scientists, Seventh Day Adventists, and Mormons, the religious practices are rather directly related to health practices. A recent study of Mormons, for example, found the majority of respondents indicating ways in which spiritual practices affected physical, mental, and social dimensions of their health (1).

Accordingly, the decade of the 80's may not be a time in which health is seen primarily as spiritual; but it should be a time in which the spiritual is more readily accepted, for some people, as an important— perhaps *the* important—dimension. For these people, the spirit is a part of both wellness and of illness and disability. Therefore it can be utilized in the healing processes, in the restoration to health.

Holistic Medicine

Positive, holistic health is the quality of functioning of the total person (including the spirit) in a total environment (including other spirits, even a guiding spirit). In addition, there is the movement called holistic medicine, which deals with departures from health in a holistic perspective. There should be some developing relationship between these two philosophically related movements.

A Model—Wellsprings

For some people learning a concept is made easier by a model. If it is to be more than just academic learning, however, the model must be one that can be recalled. Therefore it must be complex enough to represent the concept and yet simple enough to be remembered, in words and symbols. I developed the following model during the latter part of the 70's. Although there is no prediction that this particular model will become a fixture for the teaching of holistic health in the 80's, some variations of it should give focus to teaching and learning.

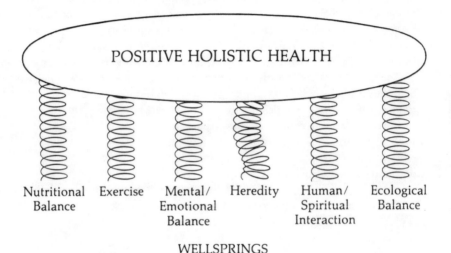

WELLSPRINGS

Health is the quality of functioning which has certain *wellsprings*. The model presents six wellsprings, five of them as coiled springs symbolizing a moving, dynamic quality, for health is a rhythmic process rather than a solid, constant state. As a term, *wellspring* means "a fount, a source of abundant supply." Broken down, *well* is a synonym for healthy, while *spring* means "to be resilient" and "to grow and develop" —abundant symbolism.

Nutritional Balance. This wellspring represents a number of balances, but chiefly a proper balance of nutrients, simplified by the recommendations of servings from the four food groups. A prime need for growth and continued health is sufficient, but not excess, protein—either complete proteins (meat, fish, eggs, poultry, milk) or as a good balance of incomplete proteins (vegetable sources).

The next decade will see a need for ever new balances of additives in food, balances of preserving, coloring, and protecting with chemicals that have other potential effects in the human body. Thus the food chemists in both camps should be kept rather busy.

For there will continue to be "camps" in relation to food and nutrition, mainly the one favoring natural, simple organic foods and the one supporting the desirability of chemicals in the growing and processing of foods—the commercial food industry. Each will have advocates with differing approaches. Each will have scientists and scientific findings that counter one another, making it difficult for the consumer. The organic, natural food movement will grow, but it will not dominate the food scene. More people will grow some of their food in backyard gardens and on urban and suburban "farms," but there will be no mass movement, only a moderating effect. Although some people will advocate and eat simpler meals and practice fasting as a health measure, industry will continue to develop synthetic foods and offer a greater variety of fast-food services.

The 80's should see more established evidence that diet is related to illness and therefore to health. Certain types of eating patterns can foster ill health, while others can be a major factor in healing and in the maintenance of positive health. There should be some firmer bases for prescribing diets, but it seems unlikely that science will prevail, given the natural variabilities in humans and in nonsynthetic foods.

A major balance, of course, is of "calories in, calories out"—between those consumed as food and those expended in exercise. This is the link between the first two springs. The main positive emphasis should be on eating to meet energy needs and to maintain a rather constant weight with a minimum amount of body fat. Minimum fat allows the body maximum flexibility and makes most forms of exercise easier and more pleasurable.

Exercise. The main objective of this wellspring is to maintain muscle tone and to keep the respiratory and circulatory systems functioning well, all of which works toward a longer and more useful life. Developing better functioning capacities in all critical body systems is a more positive goal than preventing heart and lung disease.

The trend toward more running, jogging, and cycling, and more participation in active sports will continue but, realistically, will never be called a mass movement. During the next ten years, the energy situation may encourage more exercise. All in all, there will be some reversal of the notion that the "good life" means less and less use of muscle power, but such a trend is not likely to be major. Countertrends will accompany more automation, such as shopping by televiewer and computer, and computer-assisted learning, with perhaps little or no body movement. An important factor, then, will be the extent to which young people with established exercise programs carry them over into their thirties and forties as a normal part of their lifestyle. If exercise is seen as just a youthful fad or a somewhat irregular behavior, positive health will not be abetted by this wellspring.

Mental/Emotional Balance. Health education is concerned not only with communicating more effectively about nutritional balance and exercise, but also with motivating individuals to act in accordance with what they know. Another wellspring of positive health, then, is mental/ emotional balance. This, too, is a dynamic process rather than a state to be achieved—a process of balancing feelings and emotions with one another and with knowledge, reason, memory, and other things intellectual. It also involves a balancing of stressors so that most stress experienced can be challenging (Selye's "eustress") and the potentially harmful can be managed creatively.

This wellspring is concerned with learning, as much as is needed (and perhaps a bit more), but not more than can be managed. It involves learning about self, but always balanced with learning about others and the surrounding world. In this realm the decade ahead should develop the message that one can strive too hard to know self. Such knowledge often comes as an indirect result of working selflessly for others. "Me- first" rarely results in a good balance. But the next two chapters discuss this component of wellness at greater length.

Heredity. In the model heredity is not pictured as a wellspring that moves like the others. This is because heredity presumably *is.* It determines certain characteristics of structure and certain limits to functioning. But, of course, most of the important aspects of heredity cannot be truly known, because the inherited component cannot be separated from the environmental influences, beginning just after conception.

Still, positively, heredity is a wellspring of good health. It is the inherent capacity of an individual for high-quality functioning. Charles springs from "healthy stock," and despite the fact that several of the other wellsprings that he can influence are not particularly sound, he still functions well. He is healthy. Ginger was blessed with an equally fine combination of genes and chromosomes. Her chosen and developed lifestyle results in her other wellsprings being strong and full, and so her level of wellness is high—higher than Charles's. She enjoys truly positive, holistic health.

Probably the evidences of heredity most important for health are heart and circulatory system and lungs, the digestive system, the neurological system, and the immune system. One of my grandfathers remained slim throughout his entire life in spite of a lifelong diet that was

20

far from ideal. He worked much of his life as a physical laborer and certainly had no aerobic program. He lived most of his life before the age of antibiotics, but he managed to adapt to infectious threats quite well. Even though for a long period during his last years he had no apparent desire to live, he survived until 91—because, said his physician, he just had a "good, strong heart."

The heredity wellspring proclaims, "Folks aren't created equal." If it is short and defective, the other springs must be even better for good health. If it is long and strong, positive health can be achieved with much less effort.

Human/Spiritual Interaction. Up to the present this wellspring of holistic health has been minimally acknowledged. It should receive much more conscious credit and attention during the 1980's. It is, of course, an adaptation from the dimension of "social well-being," which represents the quality of the individual's interaction with other people and with social institutions. Such strictly social interaction is an important quality of functioning. However, this wellspring applies to relations involving the spirits of people—relations involving love, trust, integrity, responsibility, honor, and sacrifice. It is concerned with the extent to which people in a society think more of others than they do of self, and behave accordingly.

A look at American culture reveals more and more apparent acceptance of differences among people—in language, in ideas, in values, in behavior. But are we developing a more accepting society, or are most of us merely tolerating differences? The test may come in a severe energy crunch or a major economic breakdown. How many would be willing to share with others, even if they had less than they once thought necessary? This is an interesting, even a frightening, question.

The human/spiritual interaction wellspring is concerned with relations between the spirits within people, relationships that are more than superficial. For some people it will also be a measure of interaction with other recognized spirits in the world—even the universe. For a good number of Americans of all ages, a vital interaction to complete functioning is that with the Spirit of God, one that may provide guidance and direction for the flow of life. The 80's will be a time of more acceptance of these spiritual relationships affecting health—for some people. (Again, this is not a broad affirmation that health education should become more "religious," but an acknowledgment, grudging to comfortable, of an important aspect of functioning for many people.)

Mental/emotional balance is Jack's relationship with himself. Human/spiritual interaction is Jack's relationship with Jill, and Pete, and Tim, and Mr. Hodgins, and old Ms. Philips, and Baldwin High School, and the police department, and Food Fair Supermarket. Are these interactions generally positive and mutually pleasant and helpful? When they are, Jack's M/E balance is easier to maintain. So these wellsprings are obviously intertwined, like the spiritual admonition to love one's neighbor as oneself.

Ecological Balance. The final wellspring (though there is no necessary order—it could as well be first) is the acknowledgment that the functioning of each person is affected by the total ecosystem in which she/he lives, and moves, and has her/his being. It involves the quality of the air breathed, the water drunk, the soil underfoot. It is the presence or absence of and interaction with all sorts of animals, insects, and microorganisms. At certain times of the year it will be healthier to live elsewhere than in the path of such natural phenomena as hurricanes that bring death, destruction of homes and crops, contamination of water supplies, and much potential emotional stress. (On the other hand, among the survivors is the opportunity for a human/spiritual interaction that may surpass anything experienced in good weather. I still remember, with much positive feeling, that night, in childhood, following a major earthquake—the neighborhood gathered together around a campfire in the street, sleeping in cars, wondering what would happen next, feeling glad to be alive.)

To say that it is healthier to live and breathe in Aspen, Colorado, than in Gary, Indiana, or Los Angeles, California, is to say that the natural is sometimes better than the industrial. To say that it is healthier to be in an air-conditioned building in Alpine, Texas, than out on the range in a west Texas sandstorm is to acknowledge that the technological is sometimes better than the natural.

We must dispose of waste. Living and working where waste is "dumped" or accumulates—whether smoke, radiation, chemicals, trash, sewage, or manure—is not as supportive of full functioning as living and working elsewhere.

In another positive sense, ecological balance means living in pleasant surroundings. For some people this means trees and flowers; for some it means a pet dog or cat; for others it means lights and music. Whatever it may be, the environmental balance in which one "feels best" is a wellspring of holistic health.

PREDICTIONS

Content

I foresee, then, that the *content* of health education for the near future will be (1) more positive and (2) more holistic, or more a matter of relationships among body, mind, and spirit. Obviously such content affects *objectives,* and suggests that there will be more purpose in having learners think and behave positively and holistically. However, the need will still exist for certain campaigns to focus on some rather specific behavior—to do or not to do. Objectives will continue to range from those which encourage relational thinking, values clarification and application, and holistic decisionmaking, to those which seek a specific behavior (or lack of it). For example, some programs will emphasize positive health in such ways that cigarette smoking will simply seem inappropriate—a practice with too many negative connotations. But other programs will be designed to help people stop smoking, in some very nonintellectual, behavior-modification ways.

Process

Naturally, as content objectives expand or change, so will the objectives that guide *process.* The major shift will be toward teaching/learning approaches that are, in effect, learning how to learn. There will be increased acceptance of the premise that learning in health is truly lifelong, and that it is more important to master certain ways of learning than to be able to recite factual content. Small group discussion will probably be expanded as the most effective approach. After some input —from reading, lecture, or computer screen—the group will talk about an issue and then be guided to make some application. The active involvement of each learner will increase the potential motivation to incorporate appropriate behaviors into individual lifestyles. Health education will employ less didactic telling and more active participation in the learning process.

Resources

Textbooks will continue to be a major resource for educating. They will be written in ever more interesting ways, however, with learning features, pictures, and other departures from the straight text as an encouragement to reading. Films will continue to improve in quality. Although remaining a source of information, they will more often be a means of visualizing certain concepts, events, or phenomena, and a stimulation to thought and discussion. In addition, the proliferation of the technology to videorecord television programs will make some interesting and provocative educational and commercial programs available in the classroom. Finally, simple but effective visual aids such as transparencies and overhead projectors will slowly increase in use.

Cooperation and coordination between health education programs in the schools and in the community will increase. We shall finally move beyond the arena of competition. Yet there may be a new aspect of competition.

Both in schools and colleges and in some community programs there will be more emphasis on positive, holistic health. At the same time health educators working, for example, in cancer programs, anti-smoking programs, immunization programs, and hospital or clinic programs (patient education) will have either a problem-solving or a medical-model orientation—perhaps both. Some professionals will be comfortable with both positive and problem orientations and will be able to use each, as appropriate. Others will favor one (or have a position that tends to require one) but appreciate the value of the other. Hopefully, these professionals will outnumber and overcome those who see the other as a threat. The apparent need to denigrate a colleague as a defense of one's own orientation, to perceive another as a rival, is a hoary but profitless tradition. The prediction is for a profession embracing both those with positive and those with medical models. It is also a hope.

REFERENCE

1. DeFrancis, Paul Charles. "Self-Reported Contributions of Spiritual Practices to Health Among Mormons." Doctoral dissertation, Southern Illinois University at Carbondale, 1979.

CHAPTER 2

A Holistic Approach to Stress Reduction

Daniel A. Girdano

In his article "Integrated Education," Aldous Huxley protested against the "celibacy of the intellect," which he referred to as knowledge organized into a series of highly specialized academic disciplines, living in monastic cells, apart from one another, not intermarrying and not producing the children they ought to produce. Huxley suggested that what is needed is to arrange marriages or bring back to the originally married state these different departments of knowledge which have been made to live apart in isolation in their own monastic cells. His biblical parody, "That which nature has brought together, let no man put asunder"(1), urges us not to let the arbitrary academic division into disciplines tear apart the closely knit web of reality.

Health problems, especially those relating to excessive stress and tension, are not just physiological, nor psychological, nor social, nor philosophical, nor spiritual; rather, they are combinations of all these disciplines. Professionals trained to help others deal with excessive stress arousal must be well versed in all these disciplines, yet need not be masters of any of them. Let not our arbitrary scholastic definitions retard our attempt to solve one of modern society's most pervasive health problems.

Over the last decade, for health education the study of stress management has emerged as an area which epitomizes two significant holis-

25

tic principles. The first is the marriage of usually separate scientific disciplines into one unified area of study, practically applied to a unique problem. The second is a restoration of balance—in this case, the more natural balance of mind-body components.

Because stress is one of the prime health problems of this era, and probably will continue to be for the next decade, health educators should be knowledgeable about the holistic approach to stress management. Full awareness involves objectives; knowledge of content; some creative, active learning experiences (including actual practice of techniques); wise use of resources (mostly people who are successfully managing stress in holistic ways); and some appropriate means of evaluation. Important as these requirements are for educators, this chapter deals primarily with my philosophy of this area of health—to which I am now devoting full time.

SOME HISTORY AND PHILOSOPHY

History indicates that we have been in a cycle—from a state of natural balance of mind and body through a mind-dominated period and now back toward mind-body unity. These changes in approach to mind-body unity have profoundly affected our treatment of health problems, especially those related to stress reduction.

Physically, there are only minute differences between today's people and the cavedwellers. We have the same central nervous and endocrine systems—brain, nerves, and hormones—that allowed our ancestors to meet physical emergencies successfully. What has changed is the extent to which the conscious mind has taken control of the body and the extent to which our total being has been transformed into ego consciousness—logical, rational thinking that protects and preserves the psychological self. In other words, there has been an emphasis on personality or ego and a deemphasis of our physical aspects.

The ancient Greek and Far Eastern philosophies did not separate mind from body, did not even recognize differences between physical matter and spirit, or, for that matter, any differences between the inanimate and the animate. Gradually there was a change from the mind-body unity philosophy (holism or monism) to a separation of mind and body (dualism). With the dualistic philosophy of Descartes in the seventeenth century, Western culture further identified with the mind rather than with a complete mind-body organism. The human being was considered an ego carried around inside a machinelike body which was ruled and used by the mind. "Lower" animals were seen not as beings similar to humankind, though functioning on a different plane, but rather as inferior life. Indeed, as the natural environment became a resource or commodity to be used by humans, nature itself was treated as inferior, rather than something of which humans were a part.

The philosophy of Descartes compartmentalized life into special-ties—science, religion, philosophy, politics, medicine—with each seg-ment of society governed by specialists. A person was a philosopher or scientist or politician or doctor. No one person could be all, even though these activities related to each individual. It is no wonder that people grew passive in the areas beyond their individual expertise. Even the care of one's personal health was left to others. If it was important, the care must be specialized.

As the balance between the mind and the body gradually shifted in favor of mind dominance, the products of the mind (particularly technology) advanced, often unchecked. We modern humans have now become so dependent upon machines, external expertise, and a gigantic bureaucracy to run our complex society that most of our activities seem to be various forms of endless technological education, whereby we attempt to learn to use our resources most efficiently. Alvin Toffler in *Future Shock* described the rapidity of the seemingly endless changes that overwhelm us to the point of producing a shock reaction to our systems.

COPING WITH CHANGE

This activity has become a preoccupation in our society. The coping styles in turn have become mind games. Thus, we have developed a vicious cycle: increased thoughts lead to stress arousal, and the conceiv-ing of ways to reduce stress merely adds to the arousal. The harder we try to reduce stress, the more stress we subject ourselves to, so we try even harder. In our efforts to *think* our way out of this dilemma, we have created a condition in which the most important channel to the basic natural truths (the body) has been demoted to second-class status. We do not act as we feel; we act as we think we ought to feel, or as we would like to feel, or as others expect us to feel. But we cannot completely subdue the innate stress response that we share with the cavedweller. That vestige of our physical past is ever present as a reminder that we cannot totally "civilize" this natural creation that we are. It reminds us that we cannot conquer nature, for we *are* nature. The denial of this naturalness pits mind against body, a needless battle with no winner.

One does not have to "go back to nature" to be more natural. All that is necessary is to stop gratifying the mind at the expense of the body. Up till now we have tuned the ear to the message of the mind; now we must listen to the message of the body. It is difficult to hear, however, over the constant chatter of the mind.

Distress and tranquillity are opposites. When distressed, the mind is bombarded with stimulation of thoughts, plans, schemes, worries, constant reenactment of or mental preparation for an event. Tranquillity is quiet, peace, somewhat of a void that can be filled with a sense of feeling the self. We cannot act or create if we are reacting. We cannot "feel" the body when it is experiencing the pain of stress. The spirit cannot be free as long as it is burdened with worry—particularly about being free.

Thus, the answer does not lie in the search for new knowledge or new truths, because there are none. The fantastic proliferation of knowledge in recent centuries has not led to new enlightenment. We have not become wiser or significantly happier; and, in many respects, we are less healthy. But we are losing our health because we are losing our balance. Holistic attempts to regain that balance can help restore health. And health educators should know and teach this.

PSYCHOSOMATIC THEORY AND THE HOLISTIC APPROACH TO STRESS REDUCTION

While not all diseases are psychosomatic, almost all diseases have some mind-body involvement. The information received from the environment, the way it is perceived, evaluated, and given importance, and the way these "data" influence thought processes and muscle activity —these factors can all contribute to the development of health, or of disease. The pathway from the social environment to ill health is a complex one and involves the interrelationship of mind and body. Even positive events can produce a measure of stress when they demand change and adaptation, but most stress develops from the negative, painful, and unpleasant events of our lives. An inseparable aspect of environmental stress is the varied and complex nature of our social interactions, fraught with feelings, expectations, and often frustration (2).

At the core of the psychomatic theory lies the concept of mind-body balance or unity. Spurred perhaps by threats of ecological disaster or by innate needs to feel self-control, human consciousness is gradually turning *inward,* and people are beginning to understand the need to restore harmony to their lives. We have seen that balance between the environment and the human organism; balance within the human organism itself is not new thinking, but a resurgence of ancient philosophies

28

that centered on unity and the interrelationships of all things. The ego consciousness—defense of self—of the individual becomes secondary to a collective consciousness of all things. This is the *holistic approach* to life.

Let us stop here and reflect on this most important concept—ego consciousness. It is responsible for most of our stress-related health problems. Overcoming the ego consciousness is the only means to restore and maintain the best possible health. The dualistic philosophy—that is, the separation of mind and body—has led to the self-as-divine concept. We stress the state of the mind over the state of the body. Psychological stability seems more important to us than physiological stability. Thus, most of our activities are centered around pleasure, happiness, and ego gratification, often at the expense of mind-body wellness. In our devotion to psychological stability and adaptation, we are losing the ability to perceive real imbalance and the will to rebalance. But a philosophy of balance dictates that one cannot satisfy the mind at the expense of the body; one cannot preserve the specie by consuming other species or the environment.

Until recently in the United States, Eastern mysticism was just that —mysterious wisdom of the old masters, but not relevant to us. The Westerner, who has been taught to believe only that which is external and that which can be proven by the scientific method, has had no basis for believing otherwise. But "new" scientific facts are verifying many of the ancient teachings. The mind and body state of tranquillity became a "reality" after it could be measured with electrical instruments. The ability of the yogi consciously to influence heart rate, skin temperature, perspiration, and other autonomic functions was always fascinating, but it was given renewed attention when it was objectively measured, and, more importantly, when it was accomplished by thousands of "average" humans. Out of this recent interest have come investigations into alternative forms of treating illness. Newer types of treatment will return to a more holistic form of health care; the individual will have more responsibility for health maintenance and will be viewed not merely as an aggregate of organ systems, but as an individual with a lifestyle of habits and activities affecting health.

Passivity about our health developed both from an overreliance on health care specialists and from a lack of knowledge about the disease process. The holistic approach views the body processes as not being completely involuntary. It holds that the individual should play an active role both in maintaining good health and in treating ill health. It dictates that the ill can no longer be seen as innocent victims of their bodies, completely absolved from any responsibility for the illness.

MAPPING STRATEGIES FOR STRESS REDUCTION

To a large extent, how stressfully we react to our environment is determined by our attitudes, values, personality, emotional development, and our ability to alter the influence of the environment. Alteration involves such factors as diet and physical activity patterns, the ability to relax, and the ability to modify our lifestyles. Understanding this concept of stress makes one realize the futility of trying to deal with such a multidimensional problem with only one activity or technique. Since stress reactions occur on various levels, stress management must be *holistic*, that is, approached from numerous and varied perspectives, simultaneously incorporating the mental and the physical, as well as spiritual, social, and environmental interactions (3).

A holistic system for reducing stress and tension consists of the following three sets of strategies: (1) techniques designed to minimize the frequency of stress, (2) techniques designed to allow one to become better physically and emotionally prepared to withstand excessive stress, and (3) techniques designed to appropriately utilize the by-products of excessive stress arousal.

Minimizing the Frequency of Stress: Human and Personality Engineering

Our environment is filled with stressors; the action or behavior of people and institutions in the world become the input to each individual. As we go about our daily activities each individual with whom we interact, the people we live with, those in the next car, those we pass on the street and sit with in meeting halls, and, to some extent, those we see on television, present some manner of stimulation. Obviously, the more people, the greater the opportunity for influence. The intimacy of that contact is also of prime importance. Not only does the behavior of others become our stimulation, but if we know them well enough, so do their thoughts, dreams, and unspoken expectations become our stimulation. Likewise, people and the pursuit of life create other potential stressors—from noise pollution to competition for a seat on the bus, a place on the highway, or a position with the company. Generally speaking, a greater number of people means more complexity in social as well as in institutional organization. And more complexity generally means more stress.

One of the easiest and most effective techniques of stress management is to identify stress-promoting activities and to develop a lifestyle which *modifies* or *avoids* these stressors—activities as simplistic as altering the time of getting out of bed and the route driven to work or as complex as long-term decisions encompassing the choice of profession, mate, or life goals. *Social engineering* is the overall strategy used by an individual to willfully take command and modify his or her life. In one sense, it represents the most conscious point of intervention, but as stress management becomes a way of life, one begins to unconsciously modify one's position in relation to sources of stress through the selection of a less stressful lifestyle.

Although social engineering strategies may be simple or extremely complex (based upon the nature of the stressor), one thing is definite—virtually unlimited techniques are available to the imaginative individual.

We are a hard-working society with an industrious heritage. Half of our waking day is usually spent working; but more than just filling our hours, work supplies much of our happiness and ego gratification. However, anything done with such intensity also has the potential to influence our lives greatly and can be a source of disappointment, frustration, and unhappiness. For most of us, the stress of work supplies far more than half of our stress load.

To a large degree, the amount of stress precipitated by our work depends upon what information is taken in and what is blocked. The way in which the information is perceived, evaluated, given meaning, and the influence of these factors on both mental and physical activity are important determinants of the stressfulness of work.

Our attitudes are the way we "look" at things, the meanings and values we assign various events in our lives. And these attitudes, in combination with characteristic ways of behaving, or behavioral patterns, can be referred to as an individual's personality. The personality has the awesome capacity to transform a normally neutral aspect of one's life into a psychological stressor. Few events are innately stressful, but we can make them stressful by the way in which we perceive them. A person may alter these stress-causing attitudes, or perceptions, by first becoming aware of the attitudinal processes and then working to alter attitude formation through the process of "personality engineering." If personality engineering is effective, the perception of a particular life event is altered to the point where physical arousal is diminished or prevented.

Becoming Better Physically and Emotionally Prepared to Withstand Excessive Stress

The information being sensed from the environment is actually alerting the nervous system by two distinctly different pathways. One is conscious, voluntary, active thought processes, and the other is essentially subconscious appraisal of sensory stimulation through what is called the autonomic nervous system.

The autonomic nervous system prepares the body for any potential action which may be needed, and it does this automatically. However, action or responses themselves are conscious and occur only after the appropriate part of the brain perceives and evaluates the situation. Thus the stress response, which is physical arousal, can be elicited by conscious voluntary action or by subconscious, involuntary (automatic) activation which keeps the body in a state of readiness. If the body remains in this state for long periods the organ systems become fatigued, and the result is often organ system malfunction. The constant state of readiness to respond with the fight-or-flight response is called "emotional reactivity."

Relaxation training reinforced by such techniques as meditation, neuromuscular and autogenic relaxation, and biofeedback-aided relaxation helps reduce "emotional reactivity." Not only does relaxation training promote voluntary control over some central nervous system activities associated with arousal, it promotes a quiet sense of control which eventually influences attitudes, perception, and behavior. Relaxation training will foster interaction with our inner selves. As a result, we will learn by actual feeling (visceral learning) that what we are thinking influences our body processes and that our body processes influence our thought processes. We will come to know our feelings and emotions as a part of our thinking experience. Our behavior will come more from what is within us rather than merely as responses triggered by the people and the environment around us.

Utilizing the Byproducts of Excessive Stress Arousal Appropriately

The primary stress response is fight-or-flight. This reaction has helped ensure our survival and continues to do so, as no amount of relaxation training can ever diminish the intensity of this innate reflex. Stress is physical, intended to enable a physical response to a physical threat; however, any threat, physical or symbolic, can bring about this response. Once the stimulation of the event penetrates the psychological defenses, the body prepares for action. Increased hormonal secretion, cardiovascular activity, and energy supply signify a state of stress, a state of extreme readiness to act as soon as the voluntary control centers decide the form of the action, which in many social situations is really no action at all. Usually the threat is not real, but holds only symbolic significance —our lives are not in danger, only our egos. Physical action is not warranted and must be subdued, but for the body organs it is too late—what took only minutes to start will take hours to undo. The stress products are flowing through the system and will activate various organs until they are reabsorbed into storage or gradually used by the body. And while this gradual process is taking place, the body organs suffer.

The solution, very simply, is to use the physical stress arousal for its intended purpose—physical movement. Our cultured society does not provide opportunities for killing a sabertooth tiger, nor does it allow us to physically abuse our neighbor. The most efficient use of the physical arousal is physical exercise. The increased energy intended for fight or flight can be used to run or swim or ride a bike. Thus one can accelerate the dissipation of the stress products; and if the activity is vigorous enough, it can cause a "rebound" or "overshoot" after exercise into a state of deep relaxation.

A note of caution! Exercise is itself a stressor, and competition adds substantially to the arousal level. While the stress of the exercise is usually absorbed by the exercise, the stress of competition often sets in motion thoughts and feelings that linger beyond the event and become the stimulus for prolonged emotional arousal. Although we often confuse recreation with relaxation, they are not necessarily the same. Recreation, while fun, can be stressful, and if competitive, can produce stress that lingers with the rehash of missed points, social embarassment, and self-doubt. Exercise to reduce stress should not add stress that lingers after the exercise. Ideally, it should be exercise devoid of ego involvement. Though strenuous, it should be a time of peace, of the harmonious interaction of mind and body. And in that sense, it may be the most natural of the stress reduction techniques.

AN EPILOGUE OF PERSONAL PHILOSOPHY FOR EDUCATORS

Within the complex nature of your life, the challenge is to remain natural and free and to be true to yourself while working, living, and communicating with those who demand conformity and "normalness" and who seek, even unintentionally, to lock up your energy. In the process of freeing yourself from stress and tension, you can naturally and subtly make changes in your life script as you reduce your ego involvement. You can care less about winning and losing, and, in general, competition will mean less to you. For the most part, you can withdraw somewhat from other people's expectations, and you can thus become less critical and judging of them and pay less attention to their judgments of you.

Stress is a blocker; it blocks and consumes energy. When you free yourself from stress, you create a void that can be filled with a sense of energy and power needed to risk, take a different path, throw off your fixed belief system, or, if need be, turn your world upside down to find peace, tranquillity, happiness—enlightenment. Stress is the bottled-up energy that becomes blocked when you stuff yourself into a restricted life in which you trick yourself into giving up what you truly need for nourishment and growth. When you start using any or all of these techniques, you begin to know yourself and to be directed by your inner feelings. Your energy becomes freer to power you into the natural flow of life.

Perhaps the greatest value of relaxation training is that it allows you a chance to get to know yourself. Beneath the constant surface chatter of the mind, you are able to look at yourself objectively with a sense of ego detachment and feel a sense of security and well-being. Although alone, you may feel closer to and more a part of the world around you. Perhaps you will learn to like yourself more, to feel more secure. If you know yourself better and accept yourself, you are less likely to be influenced by what others think you should be; you can forget the past and worry less about the future (and thereby live a rich today), thus reducing anxiety and becoming more spontaneous. You can cling less and love more—and feel aloneness without being lonely. Finally, you can begin to slow down and hurry less, for your destination is within you and in constant, easy reach.

REFERENCES

1. Huxley, Aldous. "Integrated Education." *Synthesis* 3, no. 4 (1979): 6–16.

2. Girdano, Daniel, and Everly, George. *Controlling Stress and Tension: A Holistic Approach.* Englewood Cliffs, N.J.: Prentice-Hall, 1979.

3. Everly, George, and Girdano, Daniel. *The Stress Mess Solution: Managing on-the-Job Stress.* Bowie, Md.: Robert J. Brady Co., 1980.

CHAPTER 3

Stress Management Education

Marigold A. Edwards

The emphasis and focus in health care are changing. An early analysis of the first federal budget of the 1980's cites "a growing recognition that future improvements in American health status are more likely to result from individual lifestyle changes than from an expansion of traditional medical services" (6). Economic pressures are forcing the issue of prevention, in which greater consumer responsibility for health is implicit. The government's major prevention effort in health is focused in the Office of Health Information and Health Promotion. Emphasizing the importance of self-care, stress control is identified as one of five health promotion initiatives for public health education (10). Exercise and fitness, improved nutrition, reduced misuse of alcohol and drugs, and cessation of smoking are the other targeted behaviors.

Young people are generally considered low-risk in terms of the small incidence of sickness and death, particularly in the 5- to 14-year age group. During this period, however, they form habits and attitudes that will determine their future health status. The need to teach more constructive and adaptive ways of behaving is therefore apparent. Because some teachers may be neither more skilled nor more immune than their students, it has been suggested that teachers of low-to-average anxiety levels would provide a more conducive emotional classroom climate. Moreover, Aspy and Roebuck found that levels of teacher self-concept, which parallel stress management skills, relate positively to the cognitive growth of students (1).

Because the theories and techniques of stress management evolved from the medical model of treatment and rehabilitation, the newer preventive and developmental applications, which have educational significance, have evolved slowly. Over the past decade stress has been vigorously researched, and the data affirms that individuals can manage excessive stress, given the appropriate opportunity for learning. The implications for teaching these skills to young people as a planned health initiative are clear. The associated enhancement of self-concept and improvements in learning and performance are bonuses, their boundaries not yet defined.

Efforts to teach relaxation in public education have been diverse, uncoordinated, and, in terms of impact, largely unsuccessful. Muscle relaxation has been taught most consistently in physical education classes. Scattered across the country are teachers who have had formal training (some with certification) in Jacobson's neuromuscular relaxation or tension control, either through direct contact with his Foundation for Progressive Relaxation in Chicago, or, indirectly, through Steinhaus at George Williams College and Michigan State University, where he furthered research, teaching, and training in muscle relaxation. After meditative techniques were banned in schools, the enthusiasm for them quickly abated; and they fell from favor generally when Transcendental Meditation was shown not to be a unique physiological state. Navigating between skepticism and opportunism, public education has proceeded cautiously in areas related to student psyches.

EVALUATION OF EDUCATIONAL PROGRAMS

Several school systems across the country have recognized that stress reduction and the enhanced self-concept associated with planned stress management strategies increase both the learning potential of students and the likelihood of healthy, more fully integrated individuals. Utilizing biofeedback training and ancillary techniques in a public school setting (the Spearfish School District in South Dakota), Engelhardt taught muscle relaxation skills as a health habit and as a means of improving self-concept (4). Educators, administrators, and parents participated in the program first to ensure a broad base of support. In a six-week training period of two hours weekly, all participants reached criterion levels of muscle tension and hand temperature control, decreased stress levels, and improved self-concept. Measures for self-concept indicated a transfer of the relaxation skills to a variety of self-selected performances such as athletics, sleep patterns, energy, and the workplace. This model program has been subsequently adopted by other schools.

In a private university-related elementary school in Oakland, California, 7- to 14-year-olds were taught "self-regulatory techniques for coping with psychological behaviors that detract from optimum performance" (5). During the 10-week, 20-session program, all students learned to reduce muscle tension and raise finger temperature at will. In addition to practice on biofeedback instruments, students were taught to integrate relaxation skills into their lives. Attendance records and academic achievement improved, as did interpersonal relationships at home and in the classroom. Headaches and tension states were also reduced. Before implementing the program, the faculty was trained for three months in order to reinforce the new attitudes and behaviors.

In Indiana the Anderson Community School system conducted a three-year biofeedback project to train teachers, parents, and selected groups of students (11). For example, when underachievers from grades 2 to 6 were trained for 12 sessions over 6 weeks in hand temperature and muscle tension control, results showed pre- to post-gains in self-concept and reading. After training, anxious students were reported to be less shy, volunteering more often in class and completing work on time. Parents confirmed teacher observations.

In a 10-week biofeedback/relaxation training study, fifty normal, healthy students reported 64 positive, classroom-related changes, including longer periods of concentration, better memory, more relaxed states for exams and speeches, and better ability to use talents (3).

Current research shows the practical applications of stress management and relaxation training to have far-reaching effects for lifestyle and education beyond health and wellness. The programs report changes in the following categories: (1) improved academic achievement, (2) higher levels of self-esteem, (3) improved athletic performance, (4) reduction of specific tension behaviors, (5) improved interpersonal relationships, and (6) reduction of smoking and alcohol intake.

Stress management training might well be conducted not only in health education but also by school nurses, counselors, physical education teachers, coaches, home room teachers, and certain other motivated teachers. School personnel who have a clear understanding of student learnings in such training are in a prime position to reinforce desired behaviors and to guide practice and application. Self-quieting, any time, any place, may well become reality. If relaxation and related behaviors improve athlete-coach relationships, can they not do the same for student-teacher relationships, and, therefore, the classroom climate?

On the college level, undergraduate, graduate, and noncredit courses are available in various departments or service units. For example, at Kansas State University, the biofeedback/relaxation program offered through the Counseling Center services several hundred students each semester through a variety of self-health opportunities: informational literature, lecture/demonstrations, miniworkshops, individual and group relaxation training, and instrument training. The University of Colorado Student Health Service, the first student health service to provide biofeedback training to students, offers a biofeedback, relaxation training, and stress management program to a maximum capacity of 400 students each year. The three major areas dealt with are psychosomatic problems, such as tension headache; phobias, such as test anxiety; and undesirable habits, such as nail biting.

TEACHING METHODS

What can the average classroom teacher do? Time is limited. The curriculum is already crowded. No money is available for equipment. The teacher has no special training. One answer to these and other problems of teaching stress management in the school setting is the Quieting Response (QR) programs developed by Stroebel, Stroebel, and Holland (9), two of whom are teachers. The Kiddie QR for ages 3 to 8 and QR for Young People 8 years and older (age division is arbitrary) consist of sequential exercises that follow the physiological principles of the Quieting Response and Reflex (8) in operable language consistent with the youngster's age and state of development. The objective is to teach children to retain this skill, the Quieting Reflex, for life, or to help the child "dewiggle the body but wiggle his marvelous mind."

To acquire the basic transfer skill, the Kiddie QR program consists of four tapes of less than 10 minutes each and 16 units of kinesthetic exercises of approximately 2 minutes each. Capitalizing on the child's penchant for fantasy, the coauthors introduce Mr. QR and his body friends, including Angry Puppy, Little Fish, Rigid Robot, Octopus, Magic Breathing Holes in the Feet, Magic Jaw String, and Mr. Fighty Fists, who live inside all boys and girls. These body friends provide the bridge to concepts of muscle tension and relaxation; flowing heaviness and warmth; slow, deep, easy breathing; stress and homeostasis, on the one hand, and control of skeletal (voluntary) and smooth (involuntary) muscle on the other—in order to reverse the stress response. A sample Kiddie QR exercise follows.*

---

*From *Kiddie QR: A Choice for Children*, Element No. 7, Book 2, by Elizabeth Stroebel (119 Forest St., Wethersfield, Conn. 06109). Copyright © 1980. Reprinted with permission.

Magic Jaw String and Magic Breathing Holes are body friends who play together. Remember how you learned to put your hand on your tummy and to breathe through the pretend Magic Holes in your feet? Let's try breathing again through your Magic Breathing Holes. (pause) Wiggle your toes. (pause). Pretend you have Magic Braething Holes in your feet. Breathe in some nice warm air through your Magic Breathing Holes, up through your feet, ankles, legs, knees, bottom, into your tummy. Remember now to let the air out of your tummy, down through your bottom, legs, knees, ankles, and back out through your Magic Breathing Holes in your feet.

Now QR wants you to close your eyes. (pause) Put your hand on your tummy. (pause) Breathe some warm good air in through your Magic Breathing Holes in your feet, up through your legs, and into your tummy. Now let the air out of your tummy, down through your legs, and out of your Magic Breathing Holes in your feet. (pause) Rest for a minute. (pause) Pretend you have your Magic Jaw String tied to your jaw and get ready! (pause) Keep your eyes closed. Very, very slowly begin to pull on your Magic Jaw String. Slowly let your mouth open like the Little Fish. Keep slowly pulling down on your Magic Jaw String. Now begin to breathe some warm air in through the holes in your feet, up through your legs, and into your tummy; now back out of your tummy, down your legs, and out of your feet. Keep taking easy, nice breaths through the holes in your feet. Keep slowly pulling on the jaw string so that your jaw feels loose. Breathe in slowly, now breathe out slowly. Breathe in slowly, breathe out slowly. Let your jaw string go all the way down to your tummy. (pause) Keep breathing quietly. (pause) Breathe in through your breathing holes, breathe out through your breathing holes. (pause) Breathe in—let your jaw go loose—breathe out. **Breathe in—let your jaw go loose—breathe out.** Let your lips feel good. (pause) Let your **jaw** feel good and **loose.** (pause) Let your face and body feel good and loose. (pause) **Breathe in—let your jaw go loose—breathe out.**

OK. Open your eyes. (pause) How do you feel? (child response) Gently **wiggle** your **jaw.** (pause) See how loose it feels. See how good your jaw bone feels. (pause) Notice the tight feelings in your face and body are gone!

OK. Do YOU KNOW WHAT YOU JUST DID? Can you guess? (child response) Well, that's a good guess! QR knows! That's right! YOU DID YOUR FIRST QR! YOU REALLY DID IT!!! And you did it all by yourself. And nobody knew you were doing it. Now QR says every time that your forehead, your jaw, your eyes, your whole face, or your legs or tummy feel tight, because you are

worried, or **angry,** or **afraid,** you can make yourself **feel better by doing your QR!**

You can do it by yourself! When no one is there! Or even if people are there. No one will know what you are doing. Isn't this exciting, secret, and special! **The QR is so easy.** It's so much fun to do. **It's so good for your body.** Let's try it again. Just for practice, let's close our eyes. Let's do our QR. It's as easy as one, two, three, four.

QR Generalization Exercise
(To the count of 1–2–3–4)

SPARKLE SMILE

1. Breathe in through your Magic Breathing Holes.

2. Breathe out through your Magic Breathing Holes.

3. Breathe in through your Magic Breathing Holes.

4. Let your jaw go loose and breathe out through your Magic Breathing Holes.

The QR for Young People program has six tapes, of less than 10 minutes each, one of which is to be used each week in conjunction with a private log. The six-second QR is practiced together and alone as many as 30 to 100 times a day. In addition, the teacher incorporates several one- to two-minute "quickies" as reinforcers during the day.

While the core technique for the adult QR is established, after testing at 1,200 institutions, the children's QR is being field-tested in Pinellas County (Florida) Middle Schools and at the Mesa School in Mesa, Arizona. The effects thus far are reflected in increased attendance and self-concept, as Engelhardt (4) reported, but without biofeedback instrumentation and with perhaps a more functional coping mechanism. Although results are not yet widely available, this technique is also being used with learning-disabled children and Head Start classes in Hartford, Connecticut; and early reports with hyperactives suggest improved classroom behavior. Following an intensive workshop, teachers are able to teach QR the next day.

An important feature of the technique is that it is learned and practiced at the very moment of duress. Each successful QR is therefore its own reinforcement. Such learning optimizes transfer of training to real life, even during sleep. Early on, the cue for the Quieting Response is an annoyance. When, with practice, the cue becomes a change in breathing signalled automatically, the result is the Quieting Reflex, which explains how the technique can work during sleep.

COMMON FEATURES IN TEACHING STRESS MANAGEMENT

While there are clearcut differences in successful approaches to teaching stress management, there are some common features. First, all require practice, or homework. As we practice, so we improve! There are, in effect, no free lunches (which is why tranquilizers are a more popular alternative with physicians and patients alike). Jacobson's muscle relaxation, for example, requires several hundred hours of diligent practice to achieve technical excellence. Stroebel asks his learners for a four-to-six-month commitment for the Quieting Response to become automatic (that is, the Quieting Reflex), but the daily commitment is only 30 to 100 six-second Quieting Responses plus a month-long 15-minute presleep practice of the longer nine-step procedure and an objective review of the day's activities. In learning, we are all on a learning curve—the more we practice, the better we will become.

Second, instruction is needed for technical guidance in "what to do" and "how to do it." Reading a book is not enough for the more complex techniques. Moreover, many watered-down versions that misrepresent the original are available. High-quality tape series such as those of Stroebel (8) and Budzynski (2) provide adequate information and instruction for the normal, healthy person.

Third, stress management education requires the promotion in the learner of a detached, general demeanor of "not trying hard," of "letting it happen," of "passive concentration."

Fourth, the effects are transient unless the learned skills are used and maintained. Moreover, many adults don't want to change any part of their self-destructive lifestyles. Some techniques have a known high attrition rate.

Fifth, these programs foster independence and self-responsibility as long as they are used. Sixth, of prime importance is the fact that these techniques do not solve our problems. We may be relaxed and yet unprepared for an exam or a speech. These techniques do not give skills we do not already possess, although they will allow us to optimize what we have.

In summary, the learning of stress management techniques involves three steps developed in the following order: (1) body awareness, in order to catch the earliest signs of inappropriate stress (we can't manage what we're not aware of); (2) self-regulation skills to dissipate unnecessary stress; and (3) integration into daily living.

The current interest in stress has generated a plethora of opportunities for its reduction, with variable effectiveness. The best hope lies in programs based on sound physiological principles that will develop a core transfer skill applicable to any lifestyle, programs that are also economical in the use of time and specialized teacher training.

CONCLUSION

As Selye said, "It's not life that kills people, it's their reaction to it!" (7). We have the option not to react with our bodies. We have a built-in resource. The body is our best biofeedback instrument, but we must learn to use it to regain our adaptive mechanism, and then use it on a 24-hour-a-day basis. The point is not to avoid stress, but to learn to coexist so that it doesn't "do one in." The mind is a health care system *wanting* to take care of the body, but it can do so only if, when we activate the emergency response system, we allow it to return to a quiescent level where, in a sense, we can automatically recharge our batteries (8).

To be effective, voluntary self-relaxation must result in a sustained restoration of the normal physiological state. It takes practice to use our built-in controls for cultivated quieting. This means homework. Making the comparison to acquiring automaticity in typing, Stroebel asks his patients to give him six months' practice for automaticity of the Quieting Reflex with one second for elicitation of flowing heaviness and warmth. It cannot be given like a magic pill; it must be acquired individually with diligent practice. The direct opposite of being stressed does not *solve* our problems, but it may relieve the tension headaches, and we may sleep better.

Many adults do not want to change their habitual reaction to stressors any more than they want to change their eating and/or activity patterns, even though such behaviors cause pain, illness, or, at best, are destructive to their quality of living. The key is motivation for and commitment to well-being. Stress management cannot promise longer life, but it can promise improved quality of life for those who choose. And isn't that what health education is all about?

REFERENCES

1. Aspy, D. N., and Roebuck, F. *Kids Don't Learn from People They Don't Like.* Amherst, Mass.: Human Resources Development Press, 1971.

2. Budzynski, Thomas, H. "Relaxation Training Program." Audio cassette, MV3. Biomonitoring Applications, Inc., New York, 1976.

3. Danskin, David G. "An Assessment of the Psychophysiological Effects of a Non-Problem, Health-Oriented Biofeedback Training Program." Association for the Advancement of Health Education, AAHPER Annual Convention, Kansas City, Mo., April 1977.

4. Engelhardt, Loretta. "Awareness and Relaxation Through a Biofeedback Program." Biofeedback Society of America Tenth Annual Meeting, San Diego, Calif., March 1979.

5. Estrada, Norma. "Educational Biofeedback: An Experimental Model for a Creative Setting." Biofeedback Society of America Tenth Annual Meeting, San Diego, Calif., March 1979.

6. "Health Education Projects Doing Well in President's 1980 Budget—So Far." *Health Education Reports* 1, no. 1 (February 9, 1979).

7. Selye, Hans. *Stress Without Distress.* New York: J. B. Lippincott Co., 1974.

8. Stroebel, Charles F. "Quieting Reflex: A Choice for Adults," Audio cassettes, Clinician's and Self-Instruction Manuals. QR Institute, 119 Forest Dr., Wethersfield, Conn. 06109.

9. Stroebel, Charles F. (Institute of Living, 400 Washington St., Hartford, Conn.); Stroebel, E. L. (QR Institute, 119 Forest Dr., Wethersfield, Conn. 06109); Holland, M. (College of Education, University of South Florida, Tampa 33620); 1978.

10. Surgeon General's Report on Health Promotion and Disease Prevention. *Healthy People,* DHEW (PHS) Publication No. 79-55071, Washington, D.C., 1979.

11. Worster, V. J., and Wenck, L. S. "Biofeedback in the School Setting." Biofeedback Society of America Tenth Annual Meeting, San Diego, Calif., March 1979.

CHAPTER 4

Heart Health Education

Betty W. Tevis

Cardiovascular disease is responsible for one in every two deaths in this country—about one million every year. Yet the age-adjusted death rates for coronary heart disease, stroke, high blood pressure, and rheumatic heart disease are all on a definite decline. This decline is due largely to dramatic advances in cardiovascular surgery and other treatment of heart and blood vessel diseases. The real key to a continued future decline, however, lies in the area of education and prevention. Extensive clinical and statistical studies of family medical history, physical conditions, and lifestyles have identified factors which contribute to cardiovascular disease, and one of the major goals of the American

Heart Association (AHA) in the next decade is to translate this current knowledge into community programs (which are described hereafter) designed to prevent and/or reduce the adverse effects of these diseases in all segments of the population.

PROGRAM AREAS

Antismoking

The evidence of a decline in prevalence of cigarette smoking among the adult population and teenage boys suggests that educational efforts are having an effect. To achieve a more marked reduction in widespread smoking among teenagers, however—especially girls—a multidimensional approach must be taken, aimed at all the significant counterforces that influence youths to smoke.

It has been shown that the awareness, manipulation, and first experimentation with smoking occur within the family in the first few years of the child's life. Yet few, if any, health education programs are aimed at this age group through the parents, even though, generally, parents do not want their children to smoke. Heart Association plans therefore call for aggressively stepped-up efforts to convince parents not only to *tell* their children that smoking is dangerous, but also to serve as *examples*. Because the major barrier is the general social acceptability of smoking in most settings within our culture, health education efforts will strive toward the creation of a social norm *against* smoking in the presence of children. The experimentation with and manipulation of smoking materials by children should also become taboo.

The school will remain the priority site for direct intervention, as most states have mandated smoking and antismoking programs. Educational efforts will address the various pressures young people face with regard to smoking, which often seem to override their knowledge of the dangers. Strategies will involve learning to resist peer pressure, understanding advertising and mass media techniques to influence smoking, and developing ways to resist the models of parents and siblings who smoke, as well as giving information on the immediate physiological effects of smoking. Although smoking education will be covered as a part of a positive health orientation in heart health education programming for the primary grades, the major emphasis in antismoking education will occur in grades six through eight, the ages when many students have started experimentation. School programs, however, will also mirror the fact that not all youngsters are equally likely to smoke. For example, there is some evidence that the prevalence of smoking among minority and low-income teenagers is greater than that of the general population. Programs aimed at these groups have been relatively few. Special studies will therefore be undertaken to identify the prevalence and determinants of smoking in these populations. The results could provide a sounder basis for smoking intervention programs.

Nutrition

The devastating nature of atherosclerosis, as well as the expense involved in its treatment, makes it imperative that prevention of this disease be a major goal of the Heart Association. Atherosclerosis is characterized by the deposition of soft, fatty substances (chiefly cholesterol) in the inner lining of the artery. This deposition leads to the formation of a "plaque," which is the primary lesion in the arterial wall.

Research in cholesterol metabolism in the body has shown that it is possible to cause significant alterations in the level of serum cholesterol in humans by dietary modification. Retrospective analysis of the Framingham data and a tremendous amount of circumstantial evidence support the hypothesis that if healthy dietary styles were instituted in the early years and maintained over a lifetime, their effects would be more pronounced and death rates reduced.

The question as to whether lowering cholesterol will delay or prevent heart disease cannot be answered scientifically for many years. For example, in families where cholesterol is elevated from birth, high cholesterol levels will not be manifested clinically for 20 to 40 years or longer.

Heart health education programs in this area will emphasize the role of nutrition in the prevention and treatment of atherosclerosis. The dietary recommendations made to the American public translate into nutritious diets that provide adequate calories, nutrients, vitamins, and minerals, and are free from known harmful effects. The presumed benefit of any form of recommendation must, of course, be balanced with the risk involved. But following the AHA diet over a lifetime seems a rather low risk, particularly in comparison with the risk of an early death from a heart attack.

Screening of families, both children and adults, will be useful in determining those youngsters at greater risk of adult atherosclerotic disease. Because obesity in childhood appears to be associated with adult obesity, and thereby with adult atherosclerotic disease, the establishment of dietary patterns which prevent obesity in childhood is important. The child who is guided to consume the nutrients s/he needs for normal growth has the best chance of developing patterns of eating that can be followed throughout life.

Programming in the future will focus on the home, the day care center, and the school. Beginning at the preschool level, nutrition education programs will offer strategies to assist young people in the development of food habits and attitudes that will make selection of a balanced diet almost automatic. Because the child's affective learning about food is strongly conditioned during the first few years of life, parents and others who influence the child's eating experiences will be the primary targets for preventive nutrition education. Parents must be made aware that they are shaping a lifetime food pattern by their influence on eating experiences during the early years. Teachers and administrators in programs for early childhood education and care are in a position to contribute to the development of the young child's food habits. In addition, food service personnel in such programs can influence the student's diet and the development of eating behavior. Future programming addressing these issues will include strategies to assist the learner in making decisions about food and will make thorough and up-to-date curriculum materials more available. To avoid duplication of effort, cooperation among the various agencies is essential.

High Blood Pressure

Control of high blood pressure is particularly vital since it is a leading risk factor for stroke, heart attack, and kidney failure. Past programs have focused more on screening than on followup and compliance. In the future this emphasis will broaden as schools and communities become more active in the implementation of programs that teach not only the etiology of high blood pressure but also allow young people "hands-on"-type practice in measuring blood pressure, experiences in health hazard appraisal, and learning about preventive measures.

Patient education in high blood pressure control will also be vital if any impact on compliance (keeping blood pressure down) is to be made. In order to accomplish this task, future programming will include the development of patient education modules and supportive instructional materials, as well as guidelines for the involvement of local pharmacists, dentists, nurses, and physicians. Collaborative efforts with the National High Blood Pressure Education Program and the National Heart, Lung, and Blood Institute will provide a variety of program experiences for those interested in working within this area. The need will be for health education on a much broader scale, certainly including health hazard appraisal and appropriate preventive measures, as in the schools.

Heart Health Education in the Young

Many cardiovascular disorders have their origin at an early age, sometimes in childhood. Research has shown that many American young people in late adolescence have already developed a high degree of atherosclerosis, and that evidence of high blood pressure can be found at an early age in some of those who subsequently develop its full-blown manifestations. Cigarette smoking, a highly saturated fat diet, and a sedentary lifestyle are the main contributors to the rapidity of this development. Future programming for young people will emphasize the need to choose the lifestyle that is most likely to lead to positive cardiovascular health. Such a determination will include deciding not to smoke, making informed and healthful food choices, maintaining blood pressure within normal limits, incorporating exercise (ideally aerobic) into daily life, and having sufficient understanding of the pathogenesis of cardiovascular disease to recognize real and/or potential problems that would require effective and intelligent use of the health care system.

The American Heart Association has always provided programming and scientifically accurate materials for the adult population, and will continue to do so with a new dimension added—programming and materials development for use with young persons. Heart health education can best be implemented as part of a comprehensive health education program, grades K–12. In this way, AHA will give support to carefully controlled studies designed to test and/or demonstrate the effects of heart health education programs within a comprehensive health education approach. Materials and learning activities will be developed to fit into existing health education curricula at all grade levels. Designed as modules for specific age groups, they will focus on the major areas of antismoking, nutrition, exercise, and high blood pressure control. They will present the skills of decisionmaking and emphasize taking responsibility for one's health behavior through a variety of approaches—audiovisuals, demonstrations/experiments, games, role playing, group discussions, and values clarification strategies. They will emphasize a central theme for each level and reinforce specific concepts through new and innovative activities. Wherever possible, support will be given to the appropriate education agency to ensure the teaching of a comprehensive program.

THE FUTURE

Heart associations continually develop programs designed to help people throughout the country. By working with community organizations, other health associations, and local, state, and federal governments, the associations help increase public awareness and knowledge, and influence public attitudes. The result of these efforts will be (1) a more thorough identification of those running a high risk for the development of cardiovascular diseases and referral to medical personnel for appropriate treatment; (2) a greater reduction of risk of heart attack and stroke through education on the effects of high blood pressure, cigarette smoking, and improper diet; (3) more extensive training in emergency cardiac care through programs to teach cardiopulmonary resuscitation; and (4) more complete rehabilitation for patients and their families after heart attacks or strokes.

As more sophisticated programs develop throughout the United States, there will be a need for more stringent evaluation to determine their effects. As demonstration programs show behavioral changes, there will be more and more replication in like communities. Baseline data collected during the 60's and 70's will prove invaluable for evaluation of programs during the next decade.

The 80's will not bring the total solution to the problems presented by cardiovascular disease. They should, however, bring a change for the better in our style of living and an increased emphasis on prevention. These concepts will be reinforced in the heart health education of the 80's.

CHAPTER 5

Consumer Health Education

Charles R. Carroll and Warren E. Schaller

It was inevitable that the efforts of Ralph Nader would have an impact on health education. As consumers became more concerned with getting their medical money's worth, and as the "sacred cow" image of physicians diminished, patients began to realize that they were significant partners on their own "health care team." Critics such as Dr. Robert Mendelsohn and Ivan Illich helped many consumer-patients reassert individual responsibility for their health status in a reaction, perhaps, to what some medical heretics have labeled our "overmedicalized" society.

If the present overuse of and overdependency on physicians and hospitals are ever to be reduced, then one of the most challenging tasks of consumer health education will be to *help consumers use health care providers more effectively.* Such an educational program should not be antiphysician, antihospital, or antimedicine. Rather, it should help reduce the unrealistic demands Americans have placed on an overburdened health care system in a frenzied attempt to "buy health."

Appropriate behavioral objectives for consumer health care include the following:

1. The student can identify specific consumer actions to promote his/her own health. Increasing emphasis at all grade levels must be placed on keeping healthy people well. Young persons must continue to be taught to eat nutritious foods, to undertake personal hygiene practices including proper dental care, to balance work with recreation, to avoid stress or learn to balance stressors, to get regular exercise and adequate sleep, to be safety minded in their activities, and to avoid the use of tobacco and the abuse of alcohol and other drugs. These actions can be taken only by the individual consumer.

2. The student can distinguish between minor ailments that can be treated by him/herself and those which require professional attention. Students should acquire some basic skills in self-care and home treatment, and be able to recognize emergency conditions requiring prompt action. Because many consumers have given up almost all responsibilities for their own health/disease/accident care, hospital emergency rooms are swamped with patients who do not really require the expert attention of physicians and nurses. Principles of judicious use of over-the-counter drugs and home remedies, the evaluation of common signs and symptoms of illness, and the application of appropriate home treatments for minor ailments are detailed in innovative publications such as *Take Care of Yourself: A Consumer's Guide to Medical Care* (1) and *Taking Care of Your Child: A Parent's Guide to Medical Care* (2). These or similar texts could serve as excellent resource materials. In addition, more acceptance of pain and discomfort as appropriate at certain times and more faith and trust in the healthy body's capacity to heal itself would be welcome attitudes.

3. The student can develop a cooperative relationship and improved communication skills with medical professionals. The physician/patient relationship should be characterized by a willingness on the part of the patient to follow professional advice. Consumers should record specific instructions in writing, immediately report side effects of drugs and new symptoms that may occur, and maintain a basic honesty about their current health practices and medical histories. If they do not understand a particular instruction, wise consumers ask for clarification. Consumer-patients should also ask about alternatives in treatment and the expense and consequences of each choice. Inquiries about risk factors and progress of treatment, and information about patients' rights (including refusal of treatment and requests for a second medical opinion) are essential aspects of two-way communication between physician and consumer-patient.

Although learning experiences to implement this objective may be potentially controversial, it appears that consumer health education has an increasing responsibility to help young persons go beyond the "medical mystique" and not only to choose their doctors more carefully, but to use them more effectively.

4. The student can analyze the variety of advertising appeals for health products and services. As long as advertising is considered the "voice of free choice," persons who use health products and services will be well advised to enter the marketplace of health with an added measure of caution. An important survival skill for all consumers in this area in the foreseeable future will continue to be Let the buyer beware.

Hundreds of health-related items and services, available without a physician's prescription, are promoted through media advertising as improving health status. On radio and television, and in newspapers and magazines, this advertising often provides information on product or services availability, benefits of and directions for use, and sometimes even cost.

Commercial ads, however, rarely provide the type of factual knowledge on which sound, logical, and objective consumer decisions can be made. Using well-researched techniques to convince consumers of their need for a particular product or service, modern advertisers promote their wares most effectively, telling neither bold lies nor offering helpful consumer information. Because so many over-the-counter drugs and cosmetics are practically identical, modern advertising seeks to create the illusion of superiority in otherwise similar products. Ads generally direct the health consumer toward a purchase decision by making ambiguous claims of exaggerated effectiveness or by selling a particular image, often based on fear of rejection or personal fault. A variety of media appeals may be used to accomplish such a goal.

A major objective of consumer health education is therefore to *reduce the consumer's vulnerability to advertising appeals for health products and services.* This objective is especially important as advertising increasingly directs its efforts toward the young and the non-English-speaking population of the United States; thus a particular amplification of how specific behavioral objectives could direct learning follows.

1. The student can identify advertising techniques used in the promotion of health products and services.

2. The student can analyze ads according to criteria, including source of the message, advertising technique used, and motive of the sponsor.

3. The student can distinguish between information in ads that is useful and information that is misleading, deceptive, and unfairly exploitative of consumers.

Learning opportunities should be varied and experiential-based. Upper elementary pupils can collect ads for various health products in order to determine which ads are most appealing to class members, and the kind of useful information they provide. Each ad can then be examined for evidence of puffery (exaggeration of effectiveness), statements with double meaning, unfinished claims, and quackery.

Junior high students can tape record radio and television commercials, and can identify specific advertising appeals of popularity, beauty, happiness, flattery, economy, rewards of free samples, expert endorsement, scientific backing, pain relief, humor, and acceptance by peers. Students can then determine which techniques are used most often and whether different ads for one type of product tend to use similar advertising appeals.

Senior high students can survey popular youth-oriented magazines for ads that contradict good health practices. They can write to manufacturers for verification of product-related claims appearing in commercials. Students can be challenged directly with information on specific brand products that conflict with their existing ideals or purchasing practices. In some instances, students and teachers can conduct classroom experiments to test the claims of various health products.

Knowledge in this area of consumer health education is a continuing need. If the schools do not provide such learning opportunities, the advertisers will have a monopoly on these influences —for, in fact, they are "educating" now!

Quackery in "Illness" Care

Consumer health deals with the utilization of our health care delivery system, often described as an "illness" care system because its primary objectives are essentially diagnostic and curative in nature.

Consumer health consists of at least two major areas, one considered legitimate, with a scientific base and a good deal of evidence showing positive, non-life-threatening results from the products and services utilized. The other, "health quackery," is negative and represents a risk or gamble to the well-being of the individuals using its products or services.

Quackery is defined as a product or service that claims it can cure a health problem that in actuality it cannot cure. It has persisted throughout the ages, the only changes being time, place, and people, and the product or service involved. Quackery persists because consumers buy, utilize, and think they benefit from the products and services offered. However, it can be diminished if consumers become more informed about its characteristics.

Suitable behavioral objectives include the following:

1. The student can evaluate quack claims and recognize many forms of quackery. Any claim to cure, especially one not accepted by the medical profession, will almost certainly include disclaimer phrases such as "may relieve." A money-back guarantee, diagnoses and medicines offered by mail, and personal, emotional testimonials are telltale signs of quackery in action. If "secret ingredients" or the names of doctors who recommend a product cannot be revealed; if leading hospitals that use a product and a research laboratory that developed it are not named, watch out because these are some of the classic signs of quackery. Fascinating accounts of the history of quackery and current efforts to combat deception in the field of health are numerous. They include such examples as *The Golden Age of Quackery* (3) and *The Health Robbers* (4).

2. The student can identify and use the consumer protection agencies available at local, state, and national levels. Since the passage of the Food, Drug, and Cosmetic Act in 1906, and including all its subsequent amendments, the federal government has been engaged in protecting the consumer. Agencies such as the Food and Drug Administration, the Consumer Product Safety Commission, the Postal Service, and the Federal Trade Commission in their unique ways protect the consumer and foster the development of new laws and regulations to help the consumer. Myriad public and private agencies at the state level, including state departments of health and consumer protection agencies, are also active in this area. The first line of defense remains at the local level, however, where better business bureaus, medical societies, voluntary health agencies, and chambers of commerce function. Yet the best defense against quackery is not laws and regulations enforced by governmental and nongovernmental agencies, but informed consumers who make the final decision not to use quack products and services.

3. The student can develop the attitude and skills necessary to become a consumer advocate-activist. Human behavior makes public disclosure difficult, but the consumer advocate knows that the unmasking of the quack is more important than personal embarrassment. This will protect others from being exposed to the quack's fraud and deceit. Quackery represents an unnecessary risk on the part of the consumer. The solution to its devastating effects lies in education—learning that leads toward wisdom in the individual seems to be vital in making susceptibility to quackery a historical footnote.

Alternative Systems of Health Care

Mention the word "doctor" and most people envision a scenario with a medical doctor and a nurse involved in a delicate, dramatic life-saving operation—or some similar image. Over one hundred different kinds of doctoral degrees can be earned from accredited institutions of higher education in the United States, and yet only a few of them are related to health care. Comprehension of the differences in all these degrees is difficult, at best, but add to this the fact that many individuals receive doctoral standing from nonaccredited or questionable institutions or call themselves doctor without the benefit of any formal institutional training. Is it any wonder, then, that the public is confused and bewildered about the efficacy of various systems of health and health practitioners? The situation is readymade for quackery, and one can easily understand why a variety of quacks are flourishing today, as they have in the past. It should be added, however, that certain of the alternative systems may have some merit and, in time, may become a part of traditional health care.

Suggested behavioral objectives in this area include the following:

1. *The student can distinguish between different types of doctors.* Young persons must be informed about the education and training necessary for licensing in any of the various health practice settings. Further, they must know and understand the skills and competencies of legitimate health practitioners.

2. *The student can evaluate various alternatives to traditional health care for possible application in the enhancement of health.* The foundation for medical science lies in the sciences, for example, anatomy, physiology, chemistry, and microbiology. Meticulous laboratory and clinical research are its cornerstones. Still, the practice of medicine is both art and science—and often much is art. It is clear that medicine does not have all the answers to health and healing. Alternatives to traditional health care are increasingly being considered and utilized.

A recent book entitled *Unconventional Medicine* (5) discusses over 100 different kinds of alternatives to traditional medicine. It is possible only to comment briefly on two of these, but they seem to be representative of the alternatives that will be considered more seriously in the 80's.

Faith Healing. As old as humanity, this practice is one of the most difficult to evaluate. The "healers" claim that faith in something will cure/prevent health problems. Millions of people believe and accept this concept, and at the same time millions of skeptics deny it. There is little doubt that faith plays a significant part in a person's recovery from a health problem whether that faith be in the physician and in science or in supernatural forces. Medicine must concede that there are curative forces that can be explained only on the basis of the supernatural. This is one viable explanation for the modern concept of psychosomatic medicine, which is an important tool in successful recovery from an illness. However, recognition of spiritual elements in the healing process does not require accepting all the claims made by some healers. In other words, we know there is pain and there is death, that arteries will break and that cancers will grow. Thus, it may not be wise to rely on faith alone in the healing process.

Acupuncture. This practice has received a great deal of publicity in recent years but, in fact, it has been used for over 4,000 years by the Chinese, who are its major proponents. It involves the placement of small needles into the body at predetermined places and depths to affect different kinds of diseases and disorders. Although the way it works and its precise benefits are unknown, early evidence shows some useful application in anesthesia. The process has some definite health advantages. Research is now underway to determine its validity and reliability. In the meantime, it is recommended that acupuncture be considered experimental and used only by licensed practitioners.

Final Word. Individuals considering the use of an alternative method of health care should weigh the risk of the treatment against its potential benefits. Their decision may be assisted by evaluating the scientific principles upon which the method is based, along with good judgment and common sense.

REFERENCES

1. Vickery, Donald M., and Fries, James F. *Take Care of Yourself: A Consumer's Guide to Medical Care.* Reading, Mass.: Addison-Wesley Publishing Co., 1976.

2. Pantell, Robert H.; Fries, James F.; and Vickery, Donald M. *Taking Care of Your Child: A Parent's Guide to Medical Care.* Reading, Mass.: Addison-Wesley Publishing Co., 1977.

3. Holbrook, S. H. *The Golden Age of Quackery.* Philadelphia: W. B. Saunders Co., 1976.

4. Barrett, Stephen, and Knight, Gilda. *The Health Robbers.* Philadelphia: George F. Stickley Co. Publishers, 1976.

5. Hill, Ann. *Unconventional Medicine.* New York: Crown Publishers, 1979.

CHAPTER 6

Nonscientific Healing:
What Is No Longer Quackery?

Adogbeji Lucky Oghojafor

From time to time, in all parts of the world, especially in the third world, practitioners of nonscientific healing (indigenous healing in all its forms, including nature healing) have been challenged and persecuted by purveyors of the medical establishment. The traditional, scientific, medical model of healing tends to see practices outside itself to be quackery. But in spite of this challenge and persecution, and in spite of the resultant power enjoyed by the medical establishment, nonscientific healing methods in health care persist and endure in popularity. The continued existence and patronage of nonscientific healing are found not only in the third world but also in the Western world.

Nonscientific healers are extant because they meet felt needs in a portion of the global population that would otherwise be largely "unserviced," healthwise. Throughout much of the world today, people still seek help for their ills from diviners, witchdoctors, curanderas, spiritualists, and other healers, often at the same time they use facilities of scientific medicine (8). The reason for this duality seems to be that three-fourths of the earth's population is emotionally and culturally tied to indigenous health care. The truth is that the science of medicine is not being introduced into the world in a vacuum. People of the world have always had their own systems of health maintenance.

This chapter examines some of the arguments used by scientific medicine to relegate nonscientific healing to the realm of quackery and some of the reasons why certain healers, in spite of persecution, have stood the test of time. It also attempts to make a case for cooperation and "learning from each other" among the forms of healing.

SCIENTIFIC MEDICINE'S DISCLAIMER OF NONSCIENTIFIC HEALERS

According to Torrey (11), the major disclaimer used by scientific medicine to relegate other healers to quackery is what has been called the "Tarzan Mentality." This mental set holds that Western culture represents the end-stage of evolution. Consequently, healers who do not base their art on Western scientific principle are quacks, because Western thought is more advanced than any other. However, both scientific medical healing and nonscientific healing are basically pragmatic—that is, both methods use what works. Scientific medicine bases its pragmatism on scientific experiments (usually with animals), then on careful clinical trials for perhaps a year or two, and then on physicians' observations of patients. Much nonscientific healing is based on observations over hundreds, even thousands, of years, with potions and procedures passed down over the generations because "they work."

If, on the other hand, healing were defined "being qualified to treat as you are treating," there would be true healers and quacks in *both* the scientific and nonscientific ranks. All healing professions are in danger of infiltration by quacks. Professional integrity and ethical behavior are continuing challenges to healers of all descriptions.

But let us return to the Western definition of quackery. In an attempt to distinguish itself from its "competition," scientific medicine has continuously relegated nonscientific healing to the realms of superstition and magic. The problem is that although Western patients value science, they still have certain superstitions and beliefs in magic or spirits. A description of the attempt to use Western medical techniques against a cholera epidemic in the Chinese town of Hsi-Ch'eng over 25 years ago brought this conclusion from the author, Hsu:

> In Hsi-Ch'eng, scientific measures must be put in harmony with local notions about spirits, taboos, and herb doctors which customarily figure in healing and preventing diseases. In America, on the other hand, chemical compounds, healers, and new ideas and goods, whether sound or otherwise, become most marketable when put forward as the brain child of "scientists" or as products of some laboratory where accuracy is allegedly measured in one millionth of an inch. It is thus not too farfetched to say that to achieve

popular acceptance, magic has to be dressed like science in America, while science has to be cloaked as magic in Hsi-Ch'eng. (2:148–49)

One of the most common reasons that the medical establishment calls healers outside quacks is its claim that nonscientific healers use harmful, even fatal, drugs. This may be true to some extent, but it sounds like the "pot calling the kettle black." In fact, as may be true for many of the stereotypes dealt with here, it is also likely that the harmful techniques of these healers are overemphasized while the harmful effects of the techniques of scientific medical professionals are underemphasized.

THE STRENGTH OF TRADITIONAL BELIEFS

From this author's perspective, the problem stems from one assumption commonly made by scientific medical practitioners; that is, as people of other cultures become more acculturated through education, they will automatically give up their traditional beliefs, world views, and theories of causation and prevention of diseases, and adopt Western concepts. But the question of why persons who have access to excellent medical facilities continue to use healers, folk medicine, and other non-rational approaches to health care attunes us to important issues about the character of the medical establishment. According to Mechanic, the common answer heard in medical settings is that such persons do so because they are superstitious and ignorant, and that as people become more exposed to Western culture through education, they will give up beliefs that make them seek these other healing methods (7). Studies carried out by Anumonye (1), Lambo (3), and Oghojafor (9) have indicated this is not always the case.

In this author's study of Nigerian students who have had extended exposure to Western culture through education, the primary purpose was to identify the types of treatment preferred for the mental health problem called, in Nigeria, "Brain Fag Syndrome" (BFS). Data were collected through a questionnaire personally administered to the Nigerian students at Southern Illinois University at Carbondale; University of Illinois, Urbana; Indiana State University, Terre Haute; Iowa State University, Ames; and Texas Southern University, Houston. Of the 188 Nigerian students responding to the questionnaire, frequency distribution of preference for use of mental health practitioners indicated that if the student respondents should experience BFS, 21.3 percent would prefer psychiatric treatment, 22.9 percent would prefer traditional healing services, and 55.3 percent would prefer both psychiatric and traditional healing services simultaneously. The implication of these findings is that within this sample, even those Nigerians who seem to have moved away from a traditional way of life still retain a measure of belief in the effectiveness of traditional healing methods for mental health problems such as BFS (9).

In fact, Torrey's comment on psychotherapy seems to be true of health care in general: "Too much energy is presently invested in efforts to distinguish and promote particular brands and not enough in looking at the process itself" (11:193).

APPRECIATING THE WORLD VIEWS AND PRACTICES OF OTHER CULTURES

The intolerance of medical science toward other healing and curing professions has hindered the acceptance of scientific medicine in most folk societies holding world views that are non-Western. To these people, scientific medicine is new and unfamiliar. To these people, scientific medicine does not directly relate intervention to the perceived etiology of the commonest health problems. This intolerance has also blinded the medical purists in recognizing the values of other curing and healing techniques as they exist in folk societies. This is true not only in Africa but all over the world.

Explaining the problem of acceptability of scientific medicine in folk societies, Madsen noted that more than 75 per cent of the population of Hidalgo County, Texas, is of Mexican descent (6). Today, this population is characterized by an increasing rate of acculturation of certain aspects of Anglo-American patterns of behavior, resulting in a threat to its social and cultural conditions and producing psychological stress. According to the author, in such a situation one would expect to find these Mexican-Americans relying heavily on medical and psychiatric resources. Contrary to this expectation, most of the Mexican-American in need of help for social maladjustment seek the services of the folk healers. They do so because of the beliefs about causation and intervention in health problems they share with the folk healers. Like Africans, Indians, and other groups, conservative Mexican-Americans believe most sickness is the natural effect of some imbalance in the community. These people do not regard health as an isolated phenomenon, but see it as a reflection of the the integration of the community (5).

Unlike Western thought, which defines illness in terms of specific etiology, most third world people conceive of illness as a disruption in the natural order of things—of the harmony among mind, body, the individual, the family, the community, and the spirit world. Any physical imbalance in these components is believed to result in natural disease, which, culture-bound as it seems, is believed to be beyond the scope of scientific medicine.

Case Accounts

After spending 17 months studying 46 Nigerian (Yoruba) traditional healers, the Canadian psychiatrist Prince concluded that "Western psychiatric techniques are not demonstrably superior to many indigenous Yoruba practices." He reported the unsuccessful treatment, with chlorpromazine and a sedative, of a man with psychoticlike symptoms for six months. Finally he referred the patient to a native doctor, who subjected the patient to a series of sacrifice sessions by a babalawo (native doctor) and then initiated him into a divination cult. According to Prince, the patient recovered and had no further relapses (10).

Many case accounts in the literature show the superiority of one form of treatment over all others—or of one over another. Some, showing the superiority of traditional healers over scientific medicine, contain instances of poor diagnosis or unwise treatment by a medical doctor and, hence, the greater success of the traditional. This is reality. "Scientific medicine" is practiced by many individual physicians, some of whom are not as good as the medical establishment says they are.

APPRECIATING OTHER CULTURAL VALUES AND HEALTH

One way to appreciate the contribution that cultural beliefs, values, and practices of other countries can make to health services is for all people to have an open mind toward all practices and values that have helped to promote good health for many past centuries. Holistic health involves a view of therapeutic intervention as the reciprocal interactions between individuals and their lifestyles, the cultural sanctions, and the assumptive world within which they seek fulfillment. This is the modus operandi of traditional and other nonscientific forms of healing. Studies have indicated that traditional healing is a method of healing that understands the relationship of the individual to the society and then applies that understanding.

Concepts of health within the framework of indigenous cultures are more social than biological. For people in some of these cultures, there is an apparent reciprocity between mind, spirit, social group, and body. Health is not an isolated phenomenon but part of the entire magico-religious fabric. This framework gives traditional medicine a more holistic outlook. It is an attempt to heal the "whole person." For example, Madsen observed that hospitalization is usually dreaded and resisted in the lower Rio Grande Valley where families are regarded as morally delinquent if they surrender their members to hospital treatment (6). According to his study, it is far preferable to die at home surrounded by one's family and "at peace with God" than in a hospital. Lambo states that one of the values of the traditional healing approach is that the person is not seen as a sick patient but is still valued as a person within the cultural norms (4). He explains further that certain practices with an obvious therapeutic tinge are present in many indigenous cultures, and certain factors in the traditional environment which act as powerful buffers against social pressures and conflicts consequently promote good health, especially mental health.

Herbal Medicine

A large part of traditional healing the world over is herbal medicine. For example, one family of herbs with healing properties has been identified in Africa, South America, India, China, and the Eastern Mediterranean. In Nigeria, the chewing stick has been found to have properties that can reverse sickle cell anemia to normal; in Egypt, a particular plant used as a diuretic helps in the expulsion of small stones from the urinary tract; also in Egypt, a leaf used with a root bark is found effective against bronchial asthma (12).

Chiropractic

Another nonscientific healing technique that has generally received nothing but scorn from the medical establishment is chiropractic—a healing art that does not employ drugs or surgery. In spite of some insurance support of this technique, an increasing number of chiropractors and patients and many continuing chiropractic colleges in the United States (whose existence would seem to testify to the role chiropractic can play in the health care scene) remain shut out of the medical mainstream. There are now, however, certain prospects in the United States for some form of accommodation of chiropractors into the legitimate health care team because their healing technique is gradually being recognized as an effective treatment for certain musculoskeletal ailments.

A Message for Health Education

From the perspective of health education, the values and practices of the non-Western cultures, exemplified in nonscientific health care, are vast resources to be tapped for the overall improvement of world health. The fact is, in many areas, especially in the third world, few or no medical services are available. The health services that exist are provided by healers of various kinds. Certain values, value systems, and standards of excellence appropriate in one part of the world may not necessarily be appropriate in another. But more important than the question of international prestige and recognition is the relevance of the institution to the problems and conditions in its own country.

Because the third world cannot afford the building and administration of huge medical institutions, it becomes a necessity to explore all possible avenues for the most effective, economical, and culturally acceptable methods of health care. Thus it is important to recognize the presence of folk healers in all cultures, to determine those health problems they are adept at solving (and those they cannot), and to make efforts to understand the factors that influence the selection of a healer. Among the benefits of traditional healing are its sacred character, its social control functions, and, above all, its meaning in moral terms. Nevertheless, this type of healing is the most neglected human resource in health care services, although it is probably the least expensive.

THE GOAL: TO BE COMPLEMENTARY

In this era of holistic health, the reality of alternative lifestyles and patterns of healing that have functioned well over the centuries must be confronted. Studies have indicated cases of health problems in which nonscientific healers succeed where medical science fails. This is not to say that one is superior to the other. Rather, it means that scientific medical healing and the nonscientific healing methods should complement each other, for, obviously, each has something novel and beneficial to lend the other. If proper research is conducted into traditional healing, especially the herbal aspects, many wonderful substances may be produced to fill the gap created by the inadequacy of synthetic drugs.

There is a need for all of us who are involved in the healing and caring professions to stretch our minds in order to do a better job at our basic professional mission. There has been too much nearsightedness in undervaluing the contributions of other cultures to scientific medicine. Now that the world is becoming smaller through technological advances, there is a need to take a closer and more careful look at practices, values, and beliefs of other cultures for their benefits to health. The time is ripe to examine the many ways that will provide the best possible health services for all humankind. The role of emotional factors, for example, in exacerbating functional disturbance is more widely recognized today than a few decades past and will be better understood within the next ten years. If it is true that diseases have both organic and functional components, as already noted, a dual approach in treatment and prevention becomes obvious. The following words of Nolan may help us appreciate the usefulness of nonscientific healing:

> Some healers offer patients more warmth and compassion than physicians do. Sure, we pass out pills and perform operations, but do we really care about the people we treat? We doctors are too busy doing other things. Most physicians don't have the human touch that healers have. We doctors have in the past made the mistake of "putting down" the healers as though they, and those who patronize them, were idiots beneath our contempt. This has been a serious error. So let us admit that the healers do relieve symptoms and may even cure some functional diseases. The healers encourage patients to think positively and may, by so doing, correct a malfunction of the autonomic nervous system. (8:307)

With an increasingly international and multicultural perspective in the next ten years, health education must continue to encourage respect for scientific medical healers; but it must also urge acceptance and respect for those who bring about healing through other, more traditional, ways. The 80's should be a decade of more "learning from each other."

REFERENCES

1. Anumonye, A. *African Students in Alien Cultures.* Buffalo, N. Y.: Black Academy Press, 1970.

2. Hsu, F.L.K. "A Cholera Epidemic in a Chinese Town." In *Health, Cultures, and Community,* edited by B. D. Paul. New York: Russell Sage Foundation, 1955.

3. Lambo, T. A. "Human Needs in the Wake of Rapid Change in Africa." Paper presented at the Conference on Cultural Reactions for the Future Studies, at University of Ibadan, Ibadan, Nigeria, 1971.

4.———. "Traditional Healing and the Medical/Psychiatric Mafia: An Exclusive Interview with T.A. Lambo, M.D., by Dr. Philip Singer." In *Traditional Healing: New Science or New Colonialism?* edited by P. Singer. New York: Conch Magazine Ltd. (Publishers), 1977.

5.———. "Psychotherapy in Africa." *Human Nature* 1, no. 3 (1978): 32–39.

6. Madsen, W. "Value Conflicts and Folk Psychotherapy in South Texas." In *Magic, Faith, and Healing,* edited by A. Kiev. New York: Free Press, 1974.

7. Mechanic, D. "Health and Illness in Technological Societies." *Hastings Center Studies, Institute of Society Ethics and Life Science* 1, nos. 3 and 4: (1973): 7–18.

8. Nolan, William, A. *Healing: A Doctor in Search of a Miracle.* New York: Random House, 1974.

9. Oghojafor, A. L. "Psychiatric and Traditional Healing Modalities for 'Brain Fag Syndrome' (BFS): Preferences for Use by Nigerian Students Exposed to Western Education in Selected American Universities." Doctoral dissertation, Southern Illinois University at Carbondale, Illinois, 1979.

10. Prince, R. "Indigenous Yoruba Psychiatry." In *Magic, Faith, and Healing,* edited by A. Kiev. New York: Free Press, 1974.

11. Torrey, E. F. *The Mind Game: Witchdoctors and Psychiatrists.* New York: Bantam Books by arrangement with Emerson Hall Publishers, 1974.

12. "WHO Pushing for Traditional Healing." *Nation's Health,* May 1979.

_____ CHAPTER 7

Sexism and Ageism
Nancy Lee Jose

Prejudice! Discrimination! Most people would certainly agree that these are unhealthy feelings and practices. Health education should therefore have objectives to counter them and make for better human interaction. But the first need is to recognize and acknowledge the prejudices and discriminations inherent in *sexism* and *ageism*.

Sexism is discrimination on the basis of sex, usually seen as favoring the male and devaluing the female. Ageism is similar—discrimination on the basis of age, usually manifested as favoring the young and the middle-aged over the elderly and devaluing those who are obviously getting older.

Sexism and ageism involve stereotyping, which can be likened to a pollutant. Because we are enculturated with this pollutant, the stereotype-prejudice becomes invisible, similar to invisible polluted air. As with polluted air, a critical level is reached, and the result is dangerous to health. With sexism and ageism this level has been reached, and these pollutions are dangerous to our health/life as a community. The women's movement and the gray movement are the centers of criticism of present attitudes and values. Now health education must also get involved.

The main responsibility is to define and teach what is healthy and what is unhealthy in relation to sex roles and to aging and to attempt to affect attitudes inherent within the mores of society. This also means affecting the attitudes of school administrators, counselors, and other educators in school and community. Ultimately, it is a matter of conscience and justice so that more people in this society can reach their true potential as individuals.

In health education this issue should be dealt with both as an aspect of positive, holistic health and as a problem to be solved. Positively and holistically, we should emphasize the valued qualities found in all human beings, not only those valued most in males or in the young. Positive health involves interacting with people as people, looking for the characteristics of each, rather than assuming individual worth on the basis of a sex or age stereotype.

In the curriculum, this means attention to content and teaching/learning approaches in human sexuality and family life, in growth and development, and, perhaps, in consumer health.

We have created certain stereotypes. We must bring them to consciousness and examine them. When a male is clearly identified as an athlete, a scenario develops. Is it the same for a female athlete? Should it be? When an older woman applies for a job, is she considered as a person with certain capabilities or as "over the hill," and a female at that? The Marlboro man is a sexist stereotype, as is the young woman in black velvet, linking Scotch whiskey with sexuality. Why do we need such stereotypes? Health education should explore these questions.

Too often we see concepts of masculinity and femininity, of young and old, of healthy and unhealthy as polar opposites. We see healthy as good and positive, the clear opposite of unhealthy. But when we use the same thinking to see masculine as better than feminine and young as better than old, we are discriminating on the basis of stereotypes. Or we see a woman as compliant and passive; a woman's place is in the home. Therefore a man is assertive and aggressive; a man's place is at work. The young are energetic and productive. As people reach 65 or 70, they are defined as no longer energetic or productive. Too often "retired" is translated into useless, senile, or inferior.

Self-concept is a part of each person that continues to grow and develop throughout life. Stereotyping hurts individuals and is therefore socially dysfunctional and unhealthy for personal and social development.

"A woman's place is in the home"? No more so than a man's. Eighty-five percent of the females now in high school will go to work after completing their education. Those who marry will have an average of only 1.9 children and in their early thirties will put their last child on the school bus and probably return to the work force (if they ever left it). With a life expectancy of 81 years, a woman has about 50 years of her life still ahead in which to develop human and spiritual potential, apart from being a wife and mother. Also important is the fact that women are more frequently heading families. Single-parent families headed by women have increased by about one-third over the last decade; but, unfortunately, among such families, slightly more than a third are below the poverty level in income. Teaching about family life and about the roles of men and women in the world needs to be more realistic, more futuristic, and more positive. Women work for basically the same reasons that men do—for the intrinsic value of the work and for the money to provide better for self and family. If the society or the community does not provide a sufficient number of jobs, young people must realize that when women have equality in competing, males will be without jobs as often as females. In addition, women must no longer be the last hired and the first fired.

Another kind of stereotype arises in relation to emotional development, and it must be erased from teaching about mental health. This teaching holds that men should be aggressive, independent, and strong —and certainly should not cry (a sign of femininity or weakness). As a result of this stereotype, men tend to be emotionally inhibited and, consequently, die of heart attacks significantly earlier and more often than women. On the other hand we learn, in various ways, that women are passive and compliant, more dependent, narcissistic, and emotional. Naturally, then, they are considered not suited for leadership roles. Promoting such stereotypes helps females dominate the lower-status and lower-paying jobs, while men ascend to power and control.

As males should feel OK about not having power, so females should feel natural about exerting leadership. In another sense men should feel comfortable about expressing emotions (even those associated with "weakness") and women should be able to be objective and "tough," if necessary and appropriate.

All of these concerns should become part of the content of health education during the 1980's. But let's not pretend that changes will come without some trauma. Early in the 70's Bernard found that more married women were dissatisfied and had problems with marriage than did married men (1). (This finding is counter to most expectations, since females learn from early girlhood that the yellow brick road to happiness is paved with a diamond ring, playtex nursers, and suburbia, complete with modern kitchen and washer-dryer.) Her research also revealed that single women and married men were healthiest, both physically and psychologically. Men seemed to have a difficult time achieving well-being without the institution of marriage. Single men had high suicide and sickness rates, and divorced men remarried within two years of separation. Bernard offered a rationale for the reverse being true for women. Marriage adds jobs to the life of a woman—working outside the home, providing nurturance for husband and children, and having responsibility for housework, cooking, and other domestic chores. Husbands seem to have their needs met, while the "weaker sex" is expected to be satisfied through ministering to others (1).

The educative thrust should be to reduce sexual stereotypes. If achievement, independence, intelligence, competitiveness, and strength are perceived as basically masculine traits, women who develop them will find it difficult to feel good about themselves as persons. Likewise, if nurturance, gentleness, expression of emotions, caring, and softness are thought of as mainly feminine traits, men who express them will experience some discomfort. These behaviors will be manifested in different proportions by different people, but they should not necessarily be predictable by sex.

AGEISM AND STEREOTYPING

As there is stereotyping according to sex, so is there stereotyping according to age. The fastest growing age group in the United States is that of persons 65 years and older, who by the year 2000 may constitute a quarter of the population. As scientific knowledge extends the average lifespan, the dilemmas of the aged may be exacerbated. As a society, then, we must modify our cultural views and make it possible to "gray in America" gracefully.

Negative views of aging are predominant characteristics of our Western, patriarchal culture. Our society measures human worth basically in terms of individual productivity and power. We are a nation of doers, symbolizing energy and vigor, stereotypical characteristics of youth. If youth and youthful qualities are valued, then old age cannot be easily or comfortably valued. Further, Darwin's theory of the survival of the fittest is the groundwork for the belief in competition, rather than cooperation, for the good of all. Where does this place the retiree on the Western continuum of human worth? Some people are led to believe they are failing with age—in self-worth as well as in physical strength—which is different from the traditions of older cultures. Eastern cultures, for example, value the old person as a member of a family or of society. They also have a more natural concept of death, believing it is all right to die.

In our culture the situation may be summed up as follows: "Rather than a logical and necessary process of old life making way for new life,

Western predilection for 'progress', conquest over nature, and personal self-realization has produced difficult problems for the elderly and those preparing for old age" (2). In other words, it is not good to get old, but it is also "wrong" to die. Thus more old people live longer, not being valued by the majority of the population.

The plight of men retiring today is particularly severe. From infancy they have been taught to work for what they get and to become and stay independent. Retirement therefore becomes a symbol of dependence, but often without children who see a responsibility to care for parents. After retirement a man's advice is no longer sought, and he is usually not considered a leader. (Paradoxically, however, men in the highest positions of leadership continue on past "retirement age," making those who must retire feel worse.) Perhaps because of these other factors some older men experience impotence—another thing they used to do, but now cannot.

Men have learned their stereotype. They must be masculine, independent, and show sexual prowess. As they grow older they see themselves losing their masculinity. Why can't we help them see themselves gaining in humanness?

For women, sexism is incorporated with ageism. The standard for female beauty is a single one—a youthful, slim appearance. Any change toward a middle-aged look with some gain in weight is therefore viewed negatively by society. Consequently, most older women begin to lose self-esteem as they see this happening to them.

At the same time that mothers are teaching their daughters the importance of appearance, they are perpetuating the grooming process —applying makeup, changing the naturalness of hair, shaving, plucking eyebrows, using support clothing. Pain as well as loss of mobility is the price women pay for various degrees of ornamentation. As the ancient Chinese bound women's feet, so the Americans walk in high-heeled shoes.

> Pain is an essential part of the grooming process. . . . The pain, of course, teaches an important lesson: no price is too great, no process too repulsive, no operation too painful for the woman who would be beautiful. The tolerance of pain and the romanticization of that tolerance begins here, in preadolescence, in socialization, and serves to prepare women for lives of childbearing, self-abnegation, and husband-pleasing. The adolescent experience of the "pain of being a woman" casts the feminine psyche into a masochistic mold and forces the adolescent to conform to a self-image which bases itself on mutilation of the body, pain happily suffered, and restricted physical mobility. It creates the masochistic personalities generally

70

found in adult women: subservient, materialistic, (since all value is placed on the body and its ornamentation), intellectually restricted, creatively impoverished. (3:116)

Aging can never be an easy, comfortable process until these attitudes about bodily appearance are modified.

Women are also subject to an economic discrimination that is both sexist and ageist. More women than men live out their latter years alone. First of all, women have a longer lifespan than men. In addition, women tend to marry older men and then outlive their husbands an average of at least seven years. Many of today's elderly women have not worked or have been underemployed and underpaid. Their opportunities have been restricted throughout the life cycle by sex role, inequitable salary, and prejudice. Consequently, their retirement years are often spent in poverty. (The receipt of a quarterly dividend of $439,000 by the elderly woman who was Exxon Corporation's largest individual stockholder in 1979 is a stark contrast to the plight of most elderly females.)

There is more equality in wages among younger men and women today, but there is still a long way to go. Among older workers, however, the inequality is clear—older women tend to be the most poorly paid, regardless of their ability.

ECONOMICS OF SEXISM

Women are poor and becoming poorer (4,5). To summarize their economic condition:

1. In the United States 79 percent of the poor people are women and children.

2. Among all female single-parent households with children under 18, 42 percent live in poverty.

3. Two out of three poor persons over age 65 are women.

4. Women and children constitute 95 percent of the Aid to Families with Dependent Children population.

Between 1969 and 1976 the entire increase in the number of poverty-level families was among female single-parent households. In the last two decades, the earnings of women working full-time outside the home have actually decreased relative to men's—going from 63 percent in 1955 to 57 percent in 1978. Moreover, employment outside the home is no guarantee of escaping poverty. Although 47.6 percent of all married women and 51.3 percent of all single, widowed, and divorced women are in the paid labor force, in 1976 women's earnings were only

71

half of those of men with similar education and work history. One-fourth of all welfare mothers work outside the home, but do not earn enough to support their families. Men generally "climb the financial ladder," experiencing income increments with age. Women's financial ladders are virtually horizontal, often with decreased earnings after age 35. As they become older, many women who have experienced financial security reach dead ends in jobs or become widowed or divorced. For them, poverty suddenly becomes a frightening, inescapable reality—a condition of life rather than an isolated issue. Women's work, both inside and outside the home, is undervalued and underpaid. Considered part of the expendable marginal labor force, women are last hired and first fired. They are expected (and socialized) to be dependent on men, not on themselves, even though one out of three marriages ends in divorce. Sexism and ageism are thus a combined institution that makes women poor and keeps them poor both psychologically and emotionally, as well as economically.

IMPLICATIONS FOR HEALTH EDUCATION

One role of health education, then, is to advocate change—to be a force to eliminate these prejudices and stereotypes. Another role is to help those who are not satisfied with traditional sex roles. Some people, young and old, male and female, can be called *sex-role transcendents.* They are trying to redefine themselves as persons in contemporary society. Health education can help them adapt as they "go against" some of the structures of society.

However, the main responsibility of health education is to help individuals function maximally, whatever their value system. Consequently there is a task with *traditionalists,* also. These are people who, having examined the alternatives, feel comfortable with the traditional structured roles for males and females. They are men who want to be aggressive, make decisions, and provide for a family. They are women who are passive and compliant, who respect men, and who want to be only wife and mother. For some this lifestyle is spiritually and religiously sanctioned, often by the belief in the biblical teaching that the man shall be the head of the household. Health education has a role in supporting those who choose tradition—to help them feel healthy in their choice.

The educational responsibility is to devise ways for young people to consider the alternatives and decide how they shall be, without having to "throw rocks" at others who opt for a different lifestyle. All women do not have to be independent and aggressive. They should, however, have the freedom to choose independence or dependence, aggressiveness or passivity—or something in between.

Another educational responsibility concerns parenting. In this area health education can encourage nonsexism in child raising and affirm and demonstrate the value of the elderly as resources in a community.

A healthy school (and health education comes through the environment as well as through direct instruction) is one in which all children, male and female, are given opportunities to be leaders and to be followers, to make decisions and to act on the decisions of others. Girls as well as boys can be leaders. Boys as well as girls can be quiet. Equal emotional expression—which may prevent emotional inhibition in the young males—can be allowed and encouraged.

Let's be aware of another danger, however—the androgynous stereotype. Although it may seem ideal for all people to be androgynous —to have a balance of male and female characteristics—it can also become a mold into which all children are fitted. It may be healthiest to dispense with all these terms and the concepts they represent. Instead we should teach that different individuals will display their humanity in various ways. All must learn to accept one another and to respect individual differences and points of views. Such attitudes should also strengthen rather than destroy the family, as so many fear. The invention of the wheel (and of the family) was generations ago; and as the wheels of life keep turning, so must humans (in families) develop more fully the ability to roll.

INDEPENDENCE AND COMPETITION

These individualistic qualities, much valued in American society, unfortunately tend to devalue dependence and cooperation. We need more cooperation. In addition, we especially need to be able to value the elderly who are dependent in many ways.

The ultimate evaluation of health education, in its many forms throughout the school years, will be the relative freedom of individuals to be the kind of personality each wants to be, rather than being fit into a stereotype. It will also include valuing the characteristics and the contributions of the elderly, so that those who have retired can still be considered worthy and valuable.

The elimination of prejudices does not mean that all individuals must be alike. It means the evolution to a society where persons can choose rather freely from alternatives—regardless of sex or age—and can interact comfortably and productively with those who choose differently. As health educators, we ourselves will grow as we facilitate and guide the progress of others—students, professional colleagues, and parents—along this path.

REFERENCES

1. Bernard, J. *The Future of Marriage.* New York: World, 1972; Bantam, 1973.

2. Zarit, Steven H. *Readings in Aging and Death: Contemporary Perspectives.* New York: Harper and Row, 1977.

3. Dworkin, Andrea. *Women Hating.* New York: E. P. Dutton and Co., 1974.

4. National Organization for Women. *Poverty: A Woman's Issue.* Washington, D.C.: NOW, 1979.

5. Sawhill, Isabel V. "The Economics of Discrimination Against Women: Some New Findings." *Journal of Human Resources* (Summer 1973): 333–48.

CHAPTER 8

Education for Healthy Sexuality

Stephen J. Bender

AN OVERVIEW

Over the years, sex education has consistently been one of the most controversial content areas found in the school curriculum at any level. In any given community the mere mention of the topic is certain to create some conflict. Consequently, only a handful of states require it today. Many other states that permit sex education are careful to regulate closely how and what will be taught.

Traditionally, it has been accepted that the development of a sexually healthy young adult is the task of parents, church, and family physician rather than the school. Therefore in many schools, "education for healthy sexuality" has often consisted merely of a rainy-day film in an all-female or all-male physical education class (8:3–5, 6–7). More recently, the startling incidence rate of sexually transmitted diseases among young people has encouraged some states to promote, at the local level, hastily prepared, scare-oriented lectures on the dangers and horrors of these diseases. At the same time, in other communities, it appears that sex education has assumed a somewhat higher level of respectability. Consequently, the future may offer new opportunities for the more desirable approaches.

A PHILOSOPHY OF TEACHING FOR HEALTHY SEXUALITY

Teaching for a sex education program is conceptually similar to establishing instruction in other areas of the curriculum (1, 2, 3, 4, 5, 9). The basic instructional decisions underlying all education must be dealt with, and appropriate organization and design are necessary. Because of the controversial nature of the topic, however, the ideal, sound program of the eighties, designed to teach for healthy sexuality, must consider the following issues.

Why Teach About Sexuality?

The fundamental question underlying education for healthy sexuality is "What can we really hope to accomplish by involving students in learning experiences dealing with this topic?" There is no doubt that many programs have been and continue to be suppressive in nature. Often a hidden agenda exists, designed to influence students to accept a community, parental, and/or teacher morality, that may lack congruence with reality from student perspectives. Courses that assume this posture can achieve little success. Most contemporary youngsters simply will not acquiesce to specific and inordinately limited guidelines. Students tend to discount and minimize information laden with morality and projected in a sermonizing fashion. Such an approach, based in only one set of standards, does not prepare the student to deal effectively with a complex and uncertain world, where sexual standards continue to change rapidly.

The more contemporary and successful approach to a sex education program utilizes a far less directive approach. Ideally, the curriculum should provide students with the opportunity to assess a rather wide variety of sexual behavior, to determine how such behavior can affect society, and to judge for themselves whether or not they are ready to abide by the rewards and punishments of contemporary society. In essence, the learning experiences are designed and carried out so that the student is afforded the opportunity to establish a set of values on which he/she may base his/her personal sexual behavior. It is important that teachers assist youngsters with the task of incorporating sexuality thoughtfully and healthfully into their present and future lives. By the time students achieve maturity and leave high school, they should possess basic understanding of virtually every aspect of sexuality. It is important that they recognize the existence and nature of differential sexual patterns, so that they can interact in a healthy and intelligent fashion with those whose behavior differs from theirs. It is also important that they develop critical judgment when dealing with ethical controversies.

In summary then, it is hoped that the student who has been afforded the opportunity to experience a quality education program for healthy sexuality will be better suited to achieve the human fulfillment to which sexuality can contribute. The educated student—in contrast to one who is merely informed—is more likely to behave in a responsible fashion and to experience this most important aspect of life in a fulfilling manner (8:3–5, 6–7).

What Should Be Included in the Sexuality Curriculum?

All young people are potentially capable of experiencing both the impulses and the active expression associated with sexuality. The passions, satisfactions, and devotions that humans experience range from primarily physical to essentially psychic. The entire psychophysical sexual development is extremely complicated and demanding. It involves emotions, societal influences, parental guidance, cognitive information, personal experience, and much more. As previously stated, ideally, the end product is a fully functioning person who has achieved a healthy posture in terms of sexual attitudes and practices.

Sexual behavior can certainly be merely for immediate, selfish, physical gratification. Or, ideally, it can be experienced as a harmonious blending of physical, emotional, intellectual, social, and spiritual forces. In the long run, it is the latter approach that will contribute the most to a positive and healthy sexuality (10:441).

Consequently, the question arises, "What should be included in the sexuality curriculum?" Obviously, more is needed than merely the exposition of the facts of reproduction. On the other hand, it is inappropriate to attempt to frighten young people into being "good" by focusing firmly on the horrors of the sexually transmitted diseases and unwanted pregnancies. Simply stated, education for healthy sexuality means a comprehensive and progressive educational program that encompasses the mental/emotional, physical, social, spiritual, and cultural components of sexuality. It should be a socializing process and a phase of character education (11:372).

Furthermore, a comprehensive curriculum (K–12) is the most appropriate approach to teaching such a program. It is important that the curriculum be carefully structured with much consideration given to sequential learning experiences that are planned according to student maturational levels. As in other courses in the curriculum, the presentation format and the content will change as student knowledge and needs grow and develop. For example, it is generally agreed that students should possess a sound understanding of the biology of reproduction and the physical changes associated with puberty by the time they reach junior high school so that, as adolescents, they can focus intelligently on the fast-forming values, attitudes, and relationships which are so crucial during this period. The sex education curriculum, then, must include discussion of sensitive issues and offer guidance for students who are searching for answers.

While it is difficult to agree on an all-encompassing scope of content for this curriculum, it is possible to cite the most generally agreed-upon major topics considered basic to any comprehensive sex education program.

SUGGESTED OUTLINE OF MAJOR TOPICS FOR A CURRICULUM DESIGNED TO PROMOTE HEALTHY SEXUALITY

1. RELATIONSHIPS—Traditional and nontraditional sex roles

2. DATING—Feelings of love and affection, sexual standards, mate selection

3. GROWTH AND DEVELOPMENT—Concepts of masculinity and femininity

4. REPRODUCTION—Pregnancy, childbirth, and lactation

5. HEREDITY

6. SOCIAL, EMOTIONAL, PHYSICAL, CULTURAL, SPIRITUAL PROBLEMS RELATED TO SEX

7. LIFESTYLE—Marriage, divorce, cohabitation, celibacy

8. PARENTHOOD

9. FAMILY PLANNING—Contraception, birth control

10. SEXUALLY TRANSMITTED DISEASES

11. AGING AND SEXUALITY

12. PORNOGRAPHY

13. MASTURBATION

14. SEX FOR THE HANDICAPPED (11:376–81).

Who Should Teach for Healthy Sexuality?

Perhaps the most crucial element of a sound sex education program is the teacher. No matter how well planned, how sound philosophically, or how strong the community support for a program, the ill-prepared, fearful, or embarrassed teacher will invariably defeat the entire effort (7).

The teacher selected must possess a sound biological, psychological, and sociological background, as well as an attitude of openness and understanding. She or he must have a willingness to be honest with students and must be aware of prejudices that are not valued and not easily expressed. While few teachers possess all these qualities, there are people in every school system who have the essential attitudes and qualities and who can be trained in the area of content and methodology.

The right teachers know themselves and their subject. They can speak of sexual matters with confidence and authority and suffer no embarrassment. Students respond to this type of ease and confidence; thus an atmosphere of meaningful student/teacher interaction can develop (8).

AN OPTIMISTIC LOOK AT THE NEXT DECADE

As previously mentioned, there are indications that some communities across the nation are awakening to the need for a realistic approach to education for healthy sexuality. Such instruction should therefore appear with greater frequency in the school curriculum during the eighties, although there will continue to be problems with its development and implementation in given communities. However, many or all of the following expectations may materialize during the next decade.

Replacement of the Term "Sex Education"

In the past many terms have been utilized to describe education about sex. Perhaps the oldest term is "sex hygiene," dating back to the 1800's (6). Unfortunately, over the years, the course or curriculum labeled "sex education" has immediately attracted attention and raised suspicion. Today "family life education" has assumed some prominence. Other terms used by schools from time to time have included "social concerns," "social hygiene education," and "social-sex education." In many cases, these less controversial terms were developed in an effort to neutralize community opposition. As community support continues to grow, look for more and more schools labeling their program "Education for Healthy Sexuality," or some similar title.

To many people, the term "sex education" is synonymous with the study of the physiological facts of life dealing only with human reproduction. On the other hand, some of the other terms suggest a curriculum that is too broad and inclusive. "Education for Healthy Sexuality" more clearly indicates the objective of the ideal program and should emerge as a more widely accepted title.

Establishment of Comprehensive Programs

Over the next decade look for more new programs and, more importantly, programs leaning toward comprehensiveness. It is now apparent that the "one-shot"-type program is basically ineffective. Instruction confined to a few class periods during a given academic year affords insufficient time for discussion and does little to assist students with attitude formation. The need is for more programs that structure the material at appropriate maturation levels, K–12. However, such comprehensive programs will probably *not* be designed as free standing or direct instruction or separate courses. Budgetary restraints, which will continue to develop during the eighties, will undoubtedly lead to curriculum reduction and consolidation. Consequently, although the discussion of healthy sexuality may well become more comprehensive nationally, the packaging will more than likely be integration and/or correlation with other subjects in the curriculum.

More Community Involvement

Regulations dealing with education about sexuality will become even more restrictive, especially as states mandate instruction. Look for more and more compulsory community involvement in the development of curriculum and the selection of teaching aids. While legislation will more than likely create stringent guidelines calling for community involvement, however, look for less and less *actual* involvement of parents as the decade progresses.

Look for the curriculum to be gradually expanded to include such contemporary topics as the single parent, cohabitation, the decision to remain childless, homosexuality, the double standard, sex for the aged, sex for the handicapped, masturbation, pornography, contraception and birth control, abortion, and the sexually transmitted diseases. While great emphasis may not be placed on these topics, they will be considered in an effort to give students an understanding of the wide range of existing sexual alternatives and behaviors. Unquestionably, however, there will be continued community resistance to teaching that includes these sensitive topics.

A FINAL, PRACTICAL OBSERVATION

All the predictions about education for healthy sexuality in the 1980's *should* develop—if young people are to be comfortable with this aspect of themselves and if sexual problems are to be naturally prevented. But, unfortunately, the predictions about what *should* happen and what, practically speaking, will more *likely* happen are different. It is unlikely that any major progress will be made in the eighties in expanding the underlying philosophical premise for education dealing with healthy sexuality. Programs will continue to be problem-directed, their basic objectives to orient youngsters to the sexual ideals and standards perceived socially correct and morally right by the older community, particularly parents. Programmatic goals will continue to focus on discouraging premarital sex, avoiding the sexually transmitted diseases, and minimizing the chances of an unwanted pregnancy. Basically, these are the issues perceived by most parents and teachers to be the most important sexual needs of the developing youngsters. Content such as male and female roles, especially as they relate to the social-sexualization process and the double standard, will be dealt with after the problem-oriented education, if at all. The present basically conservative mood in this country favors the problem orientation rather than the more desirable open, positive approaches to education for healthy sexuality. But hope remains as long as many of us professional health educators continue to advocate the need to explore why we behave sexually as we do and why such understandings are important to healthier life-styles, as adolescents and as adults.

REFERENCES

1. Burt, John J., and Meeks, Linda Brower. *Toward A Healthy Sexuality.* Philadelphia: W. B. Saunders Company, 1973.

2. Dearth, P. B. "Viable Sex Education in the Schools: Expectation of Students, Parents, and Experts." *Journal of School Health* 44 (April 1974): 190–94.

3. Galli, Nicholas. *Foundations and Principles of Health Education.* New York: John Wiley and Sons, 1978.

4. Hinton, Gertrude. *Teaching Sex Education.* Palo Alto, Calif.: Ferron Publishers, 1969.

5. Juhasz, A. M. "Characteristics Essential to Teachers of Sex Education." *Journal of School Health* 40 (January 1970): 17–18.

6. Kilander, H. Frederick. *Sex Education in the Schools* New York: Macmillan, 1970.

7. Ryan, Inoe J., and Dunn, Patricia C. "Sex Education from Teachers' View Poses a Dilemma." *Journal of School Health* 49 (December 1979): 573.

8. Schulz, Esther D., and Williams, Sally R. *Family Life and Sex Education.* New York: Harcourt, Brace, and World, 1969.

9. Sommerville, Rose M. *Introduction to Family Life and Sex Education.* Englewood Cliffs, N.J.: Prentice-Hall, 1972.

10. Sorochan, Walter D., and Bender, Stephen J. *Teaching Elementary Health Science.* Reading, Mass.: Addison-Wesley Publishing Co., 1979.

11. Sorochan, Walter D., and Bender, Stephen J. *Teaching Secondary Health Science.* New York: John Wiley and Sons, 1978.

CHAPTER 9

Alcohol, Marijuana, and Tobacco
Robert D. Russell

ALCOHOL

Where We've Been

"We must teach young people the evils of alcohol, so they can avoid the dangers of this 'liquid narcotic'!" Such motivation, sincerely felt, was part of the classic temperance movement of the late nineteenth and early twentieth centuries. And this motivation spurred teaching that was the forerunner of present-day health education. It was also typical of the problem orientation that has undergirded this field for the decades until the present: there are problems with alcohol; therefore youth should be made aware of these problems; thus they can avoid them.

A Positive, Holistic Orientation

If health education evolves to a more positive, holistic orientation in the next decade (as suggested in the first chapter), the approach to teaching/learning *could* sound more like this:

> In the whole balance of life, "getting high" is one of the good, important experiences. Further, achieving this with alcoholic beverages is a way . . . not the best, but acceptable. Alcohol is a drug, true . . . but it is a domesticated drug. It is a group of beverages and

drinks which are part of the normal, good life of some people; they are to be both enjoyed and respected. It is OK to drink, but it is equally OK *not* to drink, totally or in certain situations.

If a person consumes more than one drink per hour, intoxication is building . . . and intoxication can be risky. But if intoxication is desired, a person should be aware of the circumstances and try to keep them as safe as possible. There are many alternatives to drinking, and these should be appreciated. Still, drinking is an alternative to other activities, some more productive, some less. And, importantly, it can be a part of, or a companion to, other life experiences.

Drunkenness can be a problem; its ramifications should be understood. Alcohol can be an addictive substance. Some people become hopelessly and painfully dependent upon drinking. Degradation and premature death are the results of some drinking, innocently begun. But this happens to a small minority. Most of those who drink do so without severe damage.

Back to the Present

The preceding approach is future possibility. The present educational philosophy is still mainly problem oriented. Because there is no certain way of knowing which 20 to 25 kids, from any group of 200 sixth graders, will suffer the pains of addictive or otherwise damaging drinking, there is a tendency in this society to want to keep all youth away from "it" for as long as possible. This desire may result in skewing the facts, overemphasizing the negative, even lying a little. (After all, the end—abstinent young people—is a beguiling one.) This has been the situation in relation to education about alcohol. Will it change much in the 1980's?

In health education we often feel that soon new facts will arise from research activity to make our educational tasks easier. *The Journal of Studies on Alcohol* presents new research findings monthly—each odd month 15 to 20 complete, original articles, and each even month approximately 750 abstracts of studies published elsewhere and nearly 600 titles of other published studies. This material will continue through the 1980's, but it is unlikely that any single study or any cumulative research findings will make education any simpler. Alcohol in excessive amounts, over time, can cause much damage. Yet most people who drink do not do so in ways that actually cause harm. What is the central message to young people? It just isn't very clear. We tend to emphasize the dangers in order to feel that we have not been responsible for learners who become irresponsible drinkers.

A Multidomained Objective

The central objective for the 1980's should comprise three domains:

Cognitive: To understand the effects of alcohol in the human body, from the mild and pleasant to the addictive and tissue destroying

Affective: To appreciate the values of responsible drinking and to desire avoidance of the dangers that increase with heavy, regular drinking

Action: To abstain when drinking is inappropriate and, if abstinence is not chosen, to drink in amounts and in ways that bring no harm to self or others.

Thus we shall be educating both for abstinence and for responsible drinking—a tricky combination.

It is important to emphasize that the cognitive objective given states that alcohol is an addictive substance. For some people it is. For others it is not. But there is no sure way for any individual to know which it is for her or him. (I have a son who showed rather clear alcoholic symptoms at 17; I had an uncle who didn't develop alcoholism until his late 60's.) Education must emphasize that alcoholism is an illness that *can* develop in anyone (although it *will* develop in only a small minority) and at any age—a bit of the old scare.

The Symbol

One of the difficulties in keeping teenagers abstinent is that they see drinking as a *symbol* of adulthood. They see that children do not normally drink and that many adults do. With whom do they wish to identify—with children or with adults? For most, this is not a hard question to answer. When the relevant adults in a youngster's world are naturally and comfortably abstinent, then identification with adults does *not* encourage drinking. But for the majority, identification is with drinking adults—those they know, those they observe, those they see in movies or on TV, and those in ads or commercials for various beverages.

Intoxication

Another challenge in educating about drinking involves the perceptions of intoxication and drunkenness. Educational messages usually have to come down pretty hard on intoxication, but it is a risk that many young drinkers are going to try. The feeling of being free and uninhibited is beguiling—even compelling. To say that when young people get drunk their immaturity is exaggerated makes an impression only upon the very mature—those who *could* drink with the least difficulty but who are the most likely *not* to. The troublesome reality is that the teenagers who are the most immature and irresponsible and therefore least able to drink without difficulty are the ones who are most likely to drink excessively AND *least* likely to learn much in classroom settings.

Alcohol as Drug

During the latter part of the 1970's, one objective of health education was to have alcohol perceived as a drug—that is, as a "dangerous" substance like a barbiturate or heroin. An immediate complication of such a perception is that the term "drug" is used, probably appropriately, for at least five different phenomena in American life: (1) over-the-counter medications such as aspirin, cold capsules, and cough potions; (2) prescription medicines and those given by injection by medical personnel such as penicillin, Valium, and cortisone; (3) legal medical products that are used illegally such as the amphetamines and the barbiturates; (4) illegal drugs with no regular medical usage such as heroin, marijuana, and cocaine; and (5) social substances containing nicotine or caffeine such as coffee, cigarettes, tea, cola drinks, and chewing tobacco. The majority of the population place alcohol in the last category (particularly beer and wine, without considering them drugs, in comparison with items in the first four categories). For teenagers in most states, of course, alcohol fits into the fourth category—an illegal drug with no medical use. But for adults? The objective has been to portray it as a dangerous substance. Again the dilemma—it is, but it isn't. Most people don't like to perceive themselves and their friends as "drugtakers" (as in the third and fourth categories), so the concept hasn't gone very well (except among militant abstainers who have believed this all along). Therefore, as stated earlier, alcohol is a drug, but a domesticated one— a usually friendly one available at social affairs at all levels.

Fetal Alcohol Syndrome

The major new issue in the realm of alcohol education during the latter part of the 70's (and which should continue) was the fetal alcohol syndrome. Fact: There is a continuing increase in the drinking of young women of childbearing age. Fact: There is strong, consistent research evidence showing drinking in pregnant women apparently causal of a set of weaknesses and defects in children born to such women. Conclusion: There is a need to educate about this coincidence.

Drinking is one of the symbols of liberation for some young women

—which must be dealt with in health education—yet excess consumption, before a pregnancy is confirmed or even realized, may mean a damaged baby. Female learners will have to develop real concern for others to counter "the need to be their own persons" in extreme forms. A "scare" approach seems almost appropriate here, for the probability evidence is clear. But educators must be reminded that such an approach works only with some and even encourages the harmful behavior in others who are more antagonistic.

More Comfort

For most youth, drinking is much more than an act of getting high or drunk. It is a symbolic process, with many meanings for "growing up." Education must include this awareness, ideally in some valuing activity wherein learners can discover it for themselves rather than having it taught to them.

The major challenge is to educate for comfort in situations where drinking is present as well as in those where it is absent. Beyond individual conscience, a moderate and responsible social group is the major force for moderation and responsibility. Where social groups are made up of both those who use alcohol lightly or not at all as well as those who might use it to excess, the atmosphere for moderation can certainly influence all but the pathological drinkers.

MARIJUANA AND ALCOHOL

Since marijuana is not referred to specifically in the following chapter on drug education, let it be here. Early in the 70's marijuana and alcohol were perceived by many young drug users as alternatives. "Pot is our thing . . . booze is yours." But as generational differences mellowed in the latter part of the decade, the two mood-modifying substances became alternatives and "companions." Young people could smoke a joint or drink a couple of beers, either one or both.

During the 70's there was a reasonably strong movement to legalize or at least decriminalize marijuana and, perhaps as a counter to this, a successful movement (in some states) to lower the drinking age to 18. Then in the late 70's the latter trend reversed and some states, notably Michigan and Illinois, went back to 21 as the legal drinking age. Since these trends and movements seem to have less relationship to the nature of the substances than to issues like freedom, order, and rights, it is difficult to predict what will happen in the next decade. Therefore it will be difficult to educate.

Legislation for legalization of marijuana and for decriminalization is, however, not likely. Even though the country could use the tax revenue from a legal product, experiences with alcohol and predictions for comparable problems with wider use of a legal marijuana make it unlikely that any legislature would consider more permissive enactments. This makes good education difficult. The health teacher knows that some portion of each teenage class (more with each higher age and grade level) is experimenting with or using alcohol and marijuana. Good education should help students in making responsible decisions and maintaining responsible behavior in use situations. But conservative, "safe" education must say that the only responsible decisions are for nonuse.

Teaching approaches toward alcohol will continue to be mixed, with, it is hoped, an increasing commitment to a positive, holistic emphasis (as described early in this chapter). Many approaches will undoubtedly continue to be based on "alcohol as a problem," however, with facts selected to make such a case—a more sophisticated scare technique. Some clear similarities exist between this area and the conclusions drawn by Bender in his development of "Education for Healthy Sexuality."

TOBACCO

Another symbol of adulthood for many teenagers is lighting up and skillfully and comfortably smoking a cigarette. As we enter the 80's, about one-third of the adult population are smokers—approximately the same number as upper teenage males. Adolescent females smoke less and are not so likely to be smokers, but the proportional increase in the Susans, Sharons, and Karens is striking. Smoking came to be seen as rather sophisticated adult behavior just about the time the scientific evidence began to accumulate showing it as a causal factor in the major fatal diseases of this era—lung cancer, heart disease, stroke, and emphysema. An adverse reaction to cigarette use has not been rapid or dramatic for two reasons: (1) the tobacco industry is well established and loathe to shut down because of a few statistical correlations; and (2) nicotine, the major drug substance in tobacco, is addictive, so that many smokers find it difficult and painful to quit.

Harm vs. Pleasure

Education about smoking has always been rather negative, first on the basis of its being a dirty habit—better than chewing and spitting, but not much—and causing shortness of breath and an ever-present cough. The link to killing diseases has supplied facts to use as powerful pieces of propaganda. As advertised, the main appeal of smoking is for pleasure, for something to do when relaxing. Therefore the rational argument—premature death vs. present pleasure—wouldn't be very fair if people were essentially rational about their behavior. But this culture values pleasure, and young people, in particular, are not concerned about preventing something harmful in the distant future.

The Prime Objective

The unbeatable combination for the continuation of smoking is (1) an early start, at an age when smoking is clearly a symbol of acting older, and (2) the addictive nature of nicotine, which makes the habit difficult to break, once it is established. From the third or fourth grade, health education should have as an objective for all youngsters an understanding and appreciation of these truths. If they really learn them well, then those students who *do* begin to smoke will generally rationalize that "it can't happen to me."

Nonsmoker Rights

It may be, however, that direct rational education aimed at affecting individual decisionmaking can have only a limited effect. Successful experience during the latter 70's suggests that a major focus of education to reduce smoking in the 80's will be on the rights of nonsmokers. During the 40's, 50's, and 60's, the assumption grew that a smoker had the "right" to smoke in almost any place that was not physically dangerous (such as near gasoline). But smokers don't retain much of the smoke that they and their "weeds" produce—nonsmokers in the vicinity not only must breathe it, but also carry it in hair and clothing. Today nonsmoking areas are increasing, and more nonsmokers are responding to the query "Do you mind if I smoke?" with some version of "Yes, I do." Since nonsmokers are in the majority in most settings, it is becoming less comfortable to become and remain a smoker. In earlier times young people might know that some adults would object to their smoking but their peers would either approve or be accepting. Today and in the future even fewer adults (particularly ex-smokers) will approve and more peers will overtly object.

In relation to tobacco, then, the major objectives of health education should be (1) the reinforcement of the value of not smoking in nonsmoking young people and (2) the encouragment of nonsmokers to insist on their rights to a smoke-free environment. Since "acceptance" is a powerful motive for many young people beginning to use tobacco, rejection of that behavior can be a powerful social deterrent to a damaging health practice.

MOOD MODIFICATION

Alcohol, tobacco, and marijuana are effective mood-modifying substances available in American society, with special symbolic value which make them attractive to youth. In one sense marijuana is the easiest about which to educate for it is illegal and likely to remain so; in another sense it is the hardest, because it is used by many youth who need more knowledge about it. Alcohol is illegal for most youth but legal for adults. Because most youngsters will drink eventually, it seems wiser, then, to instruct them about the responsible use of alcohol and to have some not drink than to teach only for abstinence and portray all drinking as irresponsible. With tobacco there is an analogue. Although on physical health grounds it is easier to teach against smoking, youngsters should also learn the safer ways to smoke, if this is their choice.

For an important issue with these substances is freedom—the freedom to do what may not be best for oneself. The exercise of freedom, even if used unwisely, can, ultimately, become a healthy behavior. Will it continue to be so into the 80's?

CHAPTER 10

Drug Education
Geraldine Rockett

HISTORY

To examine the future of drug education, we must begin by examining its past. Historically, drug education in the schools has been promoted by adults to stop "the evils of drug abuse" by children. During the late 1800's, for example, when opium-smoking became popular, many states introduced legislation to include anti-opium courses in the public schools (1). It has often been observed that the classic temperance movement resulted in a plethora of health education courses designed to warn children against "demon rum" (2).

The 1960's

When marijuana and hallucinogens became popular among counterculture youth in the 60's, the government once again reacted predictably. President Kennedy's 1963 advisory committee on narcotics and drug abuse submitted a final report stating that

> the teenager should be made conscious of the full range of harmful effects, both physical and psychological, that narcotics and dangerous drugs can produce. He should be made aware that although the use of a drug may be a temporary means of escape from the world

around him, in the long run these drugs will destroy him and all he aspires to. (3)

Thus began the early 60's view of drug education based on a cognitive model stressing knowledge of the hazards of drug use. Such a model made for fairly simple curriculum design and program evaluation, but knowledge proved to be no deterrent to drug use or abuse. On the other hand, a report by the Educational Research Service claimed that

Attempts to increase an individual's knowledge about drugs may, indeed, have a boomerang effect. Such attempts may not discourage or lessen drug use and may, in fact, lead to deeper curiosity and experimentation. (4)

Often the information that was being given to students was itself incorrect or biased. When rating drug education films in 1972, the National Coordinating Council on Drug Education found that 31 percent of the 220 reviewed were so inaccurate, distorted, or conceptually unsound as to be totally unacceptable; 53 percent were classified as "restricted"; and only 16 percent were rated scientifically and conceptually accurate (5). While the government poured money into drug education programs, drug abuse rose at an alarming rate. This, in turn, spawned more pro-.grams, many of which were ineffective or—worse—harmful (6).

Of course an occasional innovative program did exist. In 1969, for example, the Baltimore Public Schools developed curricula that dealt with the sociopsychological issues of drug abuse as well as with the informational issues. The program stressed strong interpersonal relationships as a deterrent to drug abuse (7). Similar programs stressing values, communication, and prevention were initiated in San Francisco (8), Glen Cove, New York (9), and a few other schools. The majority of programs, however, stressed the "horrors of drugs" approach, putting little emphasis on the reasons why individuals actually use drugs.

The 1970's

The early seventies saw a new approach to drug education which Wepner terms the "ex-addict epoch" (10). The use of ex-drug addicts to supplement or replace drug education teachers began when both teachers and administrators realized that the traditional programs were ineffective. This nontraditional approach started a move toward acceptance of more communication in the classroom, although many teachers, as well as ex-addicts, continued to rely on the same old scare tactics. On the other end of the continuum, however, several programs, notably those in Sarasota, Florida (11), and Monticello, Arkansas (12), began to provide values exploration, alternatives, and counseling as part of their drug education programs.

Some Goals Beyond Information

When examining the history of drug education, it seems clear that early programs tended to be strictly informational efforts designed to stop drug use through rational argument: "If youngsters know the facts, they won't use these dangerous chemicals." Realizing that this approach simply did not and does not work with those youngsters most likely to become abusers, program administrators have begun a trend toward focusing on the individual, along with a more realistic awareness that drug use is an inherent part of our culture. This trend is reflected in the Drug Abuse Council's 1973 identification of seven goals for drug education programs in both elementary and secondary education. These are as follows:

1. To increase an individual's knowledge about drugs

2. To affect an individual's attitudes toward personal consumption of drugs

3. To alter an individual's drug use behavior

4. To increase an individual's participation in alternatives

5. To clarify an individual's values

6. To improve an individual's decisionmaking skills

7. To improve an individual's self-concept. (13)

While drug education has typically focused on the first three goals, in the 80's it will incorporate all seven. To achieve these goals, the 80's-oriented drug program must provide a combination of cognitive (that is, factual and informational) approaches, along with affective and experiential, people-oriented, approaches.

As previously stated, the information-only approach to drug education has not been effective in reducing drug abuse behavior. There is also some question whether the affective approach would be adequate by itself. One recent study of a self-development approach to drug education found that those students in the program developed more empathy skills than those not in the program. No difference was found in drug usage, however (14). To encourage responsible drug use, as well as abstention from any use, a combination of approaches to learning should be implemented. This combination would include an information-based curriculum, focusing on history of drugs, drug use, psychological and physiological effects of drugs, etc., along with an experiential-based curriculum focusing mostly on attitudes toward drugs, reasons for use of drugs, values clarification, and decisionmaking skills.

A Wider Definition of "Drugs"

In the past, drug education programs have focused on those drugs considered "bad" by the school board, administrators, and other adults in authority in the community. Although as a society we are a nation of drug users and abusers, we are generally familiar only with the "potheads" and "junkies" portrayed on the media. Less clearly identified are the truckdrivers addicted to amphetamines, the housewives dependent on Valium, the officeworkers hooked on caffeine, or the students dependent on nicotine. Drugs that are legal or obtained by prescription, and thus sanctioned by society, are often viewed as harmless. A comprehensive drug education program will examine the entire range of drugs, both medical and nonmedical, from caffeine to heroin, including tobacco, alcohol, over-the-counter, nonprescription drugs, and what Gold and Duncan (15) have called "unrecognized drugs"—those present in everyday products such as chocolate, spices, or glue. These substances are often used recreationally, overused, or simply used inappropriately as a result of lack of knowledge. Many of us have a "Madison Avenue" approach to drugs. We are continually bombarded with messages from the media that extol their virtues: "Relief is just a swallow away"; "Why feel bad when you can feel good"; "Get fast, fast, fast relief"; "It's effective before, during, and after."

Hills comments on this phenomenon:

> For more and more people, drugs legally obtained from the pharmacist hold out the promise of instant relief for psychological pains, just as we have Rolaids in America for instant relief of indigestion and Revlon for instant beauty and youth. (16)

Students who are facing profound developmental transitions are easy targets for this type of persuasion. We must then realistically ask what the difference is between Dad's predinner martinis and Junior's preparty joints (other than the illegality of the latter). Drug education programs that ignore such questions, or worse, provide pat answers, generally will be doomed to failure in the next decade.

NOW, THE 1980'S

Content of the 80's drug education program will also focus, then, on developmental issues. Chickering (17) determined that satisfaction of seven developmental tasks would yield the greatest results during school years. They are as follows:

1. Achieving competence
2. Managing emotions
3. Becoming autonomous
4. Establishing an identity
5. Freeing interpersonal relationships
6. Classifying purposes
7. Developing integrity.

These tasks must be explored, for they compare favorably with the Drug Abuse Council's goals for a drug education program. These developmental goals can provide a clear rationale for the affective component of such a drug program. For example, adolescents need to become autonomous and develop an identity separate from their family. This need can be satisfied by doing something of which their parents disapprove, a major "something" being the use of illegal drugs; it can also be satisfied by excelling in a sport or a craft. If these alternatives are not explored or are not even available, it becomes too easy to follow the crowd into drug use. In providing alternatives, however, it is important to ensure that they contain the psychological and social elements that make drug use so popular. According to Dohner:

> . . . such alternatives must be realistic, attainable, and meaningful. Any proposed alternative must assist people in obtaining the self-understanding, improved self-image, feeling of significance, and expanded awareness of new experiences that they seek through the drug effects. (18)

Alternatives can include courses without grades, such as music, art, drama, and physical education; or extracurricular activities such as personal growth groups, meditation, religion, philosophy, camping. Any activity that fulfills Dohner's criteria would be acceptable.

Beyond Alternatives

Alternatives are only one part of an effective drug education program. Also necessary are values clarification, decisionmaking skills, and an open, caring atmosphere, where students are encouraged to explore their feelings about themselves and others. Only in this type of atmosphere can students begin to examine why they use or choose not to use drugs—whether the drug is caffeine, quaaludes, or cocaine. Values clarification can help a student make decisions concerning responsible drug use. Alternatives can provide relaxation (yoga), stimulation (skiing), higher consciousness (meditation), or other means of "feeling good." Understanding and expressing feelings can help students develop a healthy self-concept, as well as a new respect for others. Thus we can see that drug education must consist of a broad-based program combining clear, unemotional, accurate information about the risks and benefits of the full range of drugs, including both legal and illegal substances. It must also provide an affective program which would allow students to examine their beliefs and test themselves through alternative activities.

Resources

How can the average teacher be expected to provide all this in one program, however? It can be done if wise use is made of local resources. The teacher does not always have to lecture in front of the classroom as the "resident expert." It is important to remember that students can also serve as teachers and, often, some are experts in their own right. Available, too, are audiovisual materials, demonstrations, field trips, graphics, television. Other people and agencies—local, statewide, and national—can also serve as resources. The school counselor or psychologist can provide growth groups, rap sessions, or communication skills training for teachers, as well as for students. The local crisis intervention center might lecture on a typical shift or allow students to come by for a field trip. Health teachers and public health departments typically provide information on caffeine, alcohol, and other drugs. Police departments offer a unique perspective on dealing with the effects of drug abuse, as does the local court system. Most individuals working in agencies are more than willing to provide service and/or information in their areas of expertise. All it takes is a request and a bit of imagination on the part of the educator. It is also important to remember that most of our education does not take place within the classroom's four walls. Innovative educators will include newspaper clippings, magazine articles, and radio and/or TV stories in their curriculum, and will continue to use the media as a prime resource. State and national agencies such as the U.S. Department of Health and Human Resources, the Do It Now Foundation, STASH, Inc., and the American School Health Association all provide printed materials on drug use which can be invaluable to teachers. The issue in resource development is one of choosing wisely and creatively from among a wealth of materials rather than one of lack of options.

Evaluation

Once a drug education program has its goals, its content, its approach to learning, and its resources, only one question remains—Does it work? To evaluate the 80's drug program, we must go back to the objectives. Knowledge about drugs is measured fairly easily, but what about attitudes, values, self-concept, behaviors? If a student never uses drugs of any kind should he/she receive an A in the course? Do we implement nationally known psychological tests in our course to evaluate self-concept? Will the assignment of a grade itself lower an individual's self-concept? One solution to these and other dilemmas is to provide a variety of opportunities for evaluation. Students could be tested on knowledge of drugs, could write a review of a book or movie dealing with drugs, could participate in a panel or presentation on a specific aspect of drug use, could share with the class an "alternative high," etc. The key to this type of evaluation is the many available opportunities that allow students who do not do very well in one activity a chance to do well in another. The major drawback is that it is very time consuming for the teacher. Much of the evaluation (for example, presentations) can take place during class, however; thus incorporating the idea of student-as-teacher, which may result in a more open, caring class environment—the keystone of the 80's-oriented drug education program.

Behavior

This area is rather cognitive. As Duncan asserts:

> Measuring behavior through pre-and post-self-report surveys has often been used. However, issues of confidentiality and of truthfulness plague this approach. An even bigger problem with such surveys is the difficulty in making a distinction between drug use and drug abuse.
>
> Nevertheless, such surveys will probably continue to be a feature of many drug education programs in the 1980's. Whenever possible such surveys should be administered to the entire school or to an entire grade, thus reducing student concern that their responses will be identified by their teacher. If the survey can be conducted by someone from outside the school—a faculty member from a local college, for instance—students may feel even more willing to answer truthfully. (19)

Intermediate behaviors may be more accessible for measurement. If, as Duncan suggests, drug abuse results largely from use of drugs as a means of coping with stress, then increases in appropriate coping skills would be a favorable outcome measure for a drug education program.

Such skills as deep muscle relaxation and assertiveness may be much more easily measurable than drug taking (19).

CONCLUSION

Historically drug education was a collection of scare tactics designed by adults so that children would "naturally" choose to abstain from substances such as marijuana, opiates, and hallucinogens. Drug education for the 80's is actually life education. It comes from a curriculum designed to help students know themselves, their needs, and their wants, to enable them to make responsible decisions regarding drug use, whether the drugs are prescription or nonprescription, therapeutic or recreational.

REFERENCES

1. *Drug Use in America: Problem in Perspective.* Second Report of the National Commission on Marijuana and Drug Abuse. Raymond P. Shafer, Chairman, Washington, D.C.: Government Printing Office, 1973.

2. Russell, Robert D. *Health Education.* Washington, D.C.: National Education Association, 1975.

3. *Final Report: The President's Advisory Committee on Narcotics and Drug Abuse.* Washington, D.C.: Government Printing Office, 1963.

4. *Drug Education: Goals, Approaches, Evaluation.* Arlington, Va.: Educational Research Service, 1975.

5. "Drug Council Finds 16% of Drug Abuse Films 'Scientifically Acceptable'." *Drugs and Drug Abuse Education Newsletter.* Washington, D.C.: Scope Publication, December 1972.

6. Bard, B. "The Failure of Our School Drug Abuse Programs." *Phi Delta Kappan* 57 (1975).

7. *Drug Abuse Education Program.* Drug Abuse Education, Grades 5, 7, 9. Baltimore City Public Schools, Md., 1969. ED 038 660

8. Winston, S. L. "Drug Counseling Workshops: A New Resource for Schools." *Journal of Secondary Education* 44 (1969).

9. Daniels, R. M. "Drug Education Begins Before Kindergarten: The Glen Cove, New York, Pilot Program." Paper presented at the Annual Meeting of the American School Health Association, Philadelphia, Pa., November 1979.

10. Wepner, S.F. "Which Way Drug Education?" *Journal of Drug Education* 9, no. 2 (1979).

11. *Drug Education Through the Humanities.* An Overview: ESEA Title III Project. Sarasota, Fla.: Sarasota County Schools (3636 South Shade Ave., Sarasota 33579), 1974.

12. *Drug Education Program. An Alternative Approach.* Monticello, Ark.: Monticello Public Schools (P.O. Box 517, Monticello 71655).

13. Abrams, L. A.; Garfield, E. T.; and Swisher, J.D., eds. *Accountability in Drug Education: A Model for Evaluation.* Washington, D.C.: Drug Abuse Council, 1973.

14. Jackson, J., and Calsyn, R. "Evaluations of a Self-Development Approach to Drug Education: Some Mixed Results." *Journal of Drug Education* 7, no. 1 (1977).

15. Gold, R. S., and Duncan, D. F. *Categorizing Drugs and Drug Taking.* Ann Arbor, Mich.: Counseling and Personnel Services Information Center, 1979.

16. Hills, S. "Drugs and the Medicalization of Human Problems." *Journal of Drug Education* 7, no. 4 (1977).

17. Chickering, A. W. *Education and Identity.* San Francisco: Jossey-Bass, 1969.

18. Dohner, V. A. *Alternatives: One Approach to Drug Education.* Washington, D.C.: American Vocational Association, 1973.

19. Duncan, D.F. "The Acquisition, Maintenance, and Treatment of Polydrug Dependence." *Journal of Psychedelic Drugs* 7, no. 2 (1975): 209–13.

CHAPTER 11

Death Education Comes of Age

Kathleen Hoyt Middleton

PREDICTION

In the 1980's the subject of death and dying will become an accepted and essential aspect of the health education curriculum. It will be thought of naturally as the culmination of the life cycle.

Why Death Education?

A subject once unthinkable for education is now being taught in a number of schools across the nation—sometimes within an already established course in the curriculum, and occasionally as a separate course offering. Wherever it may be found, there seems to be consensus that in the recent past the subject has been avoided ("denied" in the jargon), and it is now high time that it be "let out of the closet."

"Death! What's all this talk about death when the thrust in health education is supposed to be wellness?"

"I would rather think about life, living, being happy and healthy!" Paradoxically, that is precisely why death education is being taught. Death is a very important part of *life* that affects everyone. The realization of mortality can make a significant impact on our value of life. Consider the following questions: Would you have acted differently toward a loved one in the last day or so if you *knew* that person was going to die today? Would there be something left unsaid to that particular person?

When asked the first question, most students answer "Yes!" They mention things such as "I wouldn't have yelled at my mother this morning," or "I would have told my grandfather that I loved him," or "I could have helped my dad in the yard without pouting." These responses are typical of young people. The fact is almost as sad as the actual loss. If we could understand more fully the boundaries of life, then each day could take on more meaning. Why wait until tomorrow to laugh and enjoy? Why wait until tomorrow to start that self-improvement plan in the back of your mind? Why wait until tomorrow to tell someone how much you appreciate her or him?

Although there is more openness about the subject of death in the media, proponents of death education have not been entirely successful in getting across the justification and significance of this openness. The overall goal for death education, regardless of the discipline it may be found in, is to enable the learners to live more fully once they have internalized the concept of death.

Part of Health Education

There seems to be some acknowledgment at present that education about death is needed. But where do we put it? In terms of the overall school or university curriculum, it can be found logically within sociology, psychology, medicine, nursing, theology, and philosophy, as well as in health education. If death education is aimed at improving the quality of life, which may mean reexamining one's lifestyle, or, for young people, helping design an effective lifestyle, health education is an appropriate spot. For this reason it is increasingly found within the university curriculum as part of a basic health class or as a separate health-related course, or both. It is also found in the high school as a unit, "mini-unit," or module within a social studies course, psychology class, or any of several other classes, but frequently in the health class. It should be stated, however, that as we begin the 1980's the topic is still a controversial issue in education, not yet accepted by local school districts and not usually included in elementary or secondary health textbooks. The first supplementary text on coping with death and dying for high school students was published in 1980 (1). Although conservatism is strong, the prediction is that death education will thrive.

Where Should It Go?

Because death education is quite a new part of the family in terms of health education, there has been much haste to add these units to health education curricula throughout the country. Where, however, is the appropriate place for education about death? In a separate unit? Or as part of a unit on growth and development? consumer health? family health? or accidents and safety?

Sliepcevich observed in 1968 that "Each individual is a growing and developing organism from conception to death" (2). And in 1973, Hoyman urged that students be helped "to view human life as a dynamic process extending from generation to generation and from birth to death" (3). Both scholars justify the inclusion of death education within the content of health education. They also imply that the concepts for this topic are broad-based and can and should be part of several units, major concepts, or strands.

A Teaching Plan

The School Health Education Study (SHES) designed a conceptual framework to "stand the test of time and change so that component parts would not be subject to continual revision with each new medical advance or discovery of knowledge" (4:13). Using the broad-based concepts for health education identified by that study, this author developed subconcepts for death education for a master's thesis (5). These subconcepts are offered as the necessary first step to integration of the topic into health education. Six of the ten SHES concepts lent themselves to this subdevelopment. The first is a kind of transition unit, dealing with death's opposite in growth and development—longevity.

CONCEPTS AND SUBCONCEPTS

SHES CONCEPT 1. Growth and development influences and is influenced by the structure and functioning of the individual.

Subconcept

a. Longevity affects and is affected by individual growth and development.

SHES CONCEPT 2. Growing and developing follows a predictable sequence, yet is unique for each individual.

Subconcepts

a. Death is a universal event signifying the end of an individual's life cycle.

b. Dying is a dynamic process surrounding the event of death.

SHES CONCEPT 4. The potential for hazards and accidents exists, whatever the environment.

Subconcept

a. Many deaths are due to accidents, some of which might have been prevented.

SHES CONCEPT 5. There are reciprocal relationships involving humans, disease, and environment.

Subconcept

a. Interrelationships of disease and environment result in varying degrees of health, ranging from high-level wellness to death.

SHES CONCEPT 6. The family serves to perpetuate human beings and to fulfill certain health needs.

Subconcepts

a. Death and dying affect family relationships.

b. An individual's reaction to death, dying, and bereavement is strongly influenced by the attitudes of family, friends, and community.

SHES CONCEPT 8. Utilization of health information, products, and services is guided by values and perceptions.

Subconcept

a. Values and perceptions influence the selection of products and services utilized when a death occurs.

Once a conceptual framework is established, the development of related curriculum components is possible. These other components include the following: (1) instructional objectives for each subconcept, (2) an outline of content needed for each objective, (3) a description of learning activities for each objective, and (4) a description of activities which help the teacher evaluate the student's success in completing the stated objective. The addition of these components will provide both the structure and the methodology needed to integrate death education into health education. Here are two examples of these components carried through from the conceptual framework to the specific activities in the classroom.

SHES CONCEPT 2. Growing and developing follows a predictable sequence, yet is unique for each individual.

Subconcept

Dying is a dynamic process surrounding the event of death.

Instructional Objective

The student will be able to describe the interrelationships of dying, death, and bereavement.

Content

a. Death is an event, the actual loss of life. It is the culmination of the dying process and the cause of bereavement by family and friends.

b. Dying is the individual's last growth period prior to death. It institutes a climate of anticipated loss. Family members will also experience this feeling of anticipated loss.

c. Bereavement is the realization of loss of a loved one. It is the period when family members and friends learn to live with the loss.

*d. The interrelationship of death, dying, and bereavement is associated with the concept of loss. Death is the actual loss, dying the anticipation of loss, and bereavement is learning to live with the loss.

Teaching Strategies/Learning Opportunities

a. Minilecture. Using the content outline, explain to students that "dying," "death," and "bereavement" are related by the concept of loss. This concept can be applied to other situations to better understand it.

b. Analogy. First write the words *anticipated, actual,* and *realized* on the board. Then read the following story to students, explaining that it deals with the concept of loss.

> Imagine that you and your parents have a very old dog. Lady has been a member of your household for almost as long as you have. She is the best dog in the neighborhood. She does tricks for friends when they come over, and everyone is always amazed. She sleeps at the foot of your bed and always makes sure you get up in time for school. She is a real friend. Lately, she has been limping a little and cannot play ball as well as she used to. The vet has said that she is old and has some cancer in one leg. You know she is old and now it looks as if she is very sick *(anticipated loss)*.
>
> One day when you come home from school, Lady is not at the door to greet you with her wagging tail. Your mother's eyes are red. You know what has happened *(actual loss)*.
>
> Now, you have to get up in the morning by yourself; there is no soft bark to let you know it is time. When you go into the kitchen, you look at the empty food bowls. Your mother has said you could get another dog, but there will be no dog like Lady. You will have to think a long time before you are ready for a different dog, but you think someday you will be ready for one *(realized loss)*.

Go over each part of the story with students, relating the concept of loss to death. Ask them to identify dying, death, and bereavement in the story, noting, of course, that the death and the final stages of dying in this example were not actually experienced.

c. Tell a story. Have students write, tape, or draw a story that describes a death, either of animals or people. Ask that the story be fictional to avoid any invasion of privacy. Make sure students include, this time, a description of actual dying and bereavement as well as of death. They should save stories for evaluation.

Evaluation Activity

Have students describe in written form how the concept of loss relates to their story. Collect papers and evaluate the students' ability to describe how death, dying, and bereavement are interrelated by the concept of loss. Anticipated loss relates to dying, actual loss relates to death, and realized loss relates to bereavement.

SHES CONCEPT 6. The family serves to perpetuate human beings and to fulfill certain health needs.

Subconcept

Death and dying affect family relationships.

Instructional Objective:

The student will be able to analyze physical, social, and emotional needs of the dying person.

Content:

a. Even though a person is dying, he/she needs to be as physically healthy and comfortable as possible. This may include medical and nursing care, special nutritional considerations, and a physically healthy environment.

b. Some of the dying person's greatest needs are social in nature.
(1) He/she needs people to talk to about the "unknown," as there are many fears. Someone needs to be a listener. This can be facilitated by a family member, a counselor, a religious leader, or a hospital staff member (often a health educator). Hospitals are finding greater need to provide trained staff just for this purpose.
(2) The dying person needs to feel that s/he is still a part of society. Too often, it is difficult for friends and family to face up to the fact that someone near is dying. They may stay away from the dying person because it is uncomfortable.
(3) As well as being a part of society, the dying person needs to feel that she/he is still needed by the family. A family that takes away all responsibilities from the dying person says, in effect, "We do not need you any longer to help in family affairs." Decisions that need to be made concerning the dying person should include her/him.

c. The dying patient needs emotional support. Some treatments can be disfiguring, which may leave the patient with a low self-image. Counseling that reinforces the patient's worth and emphasizes the positive aspects of the dying process is helpful. Positive aspects include a chance for families to pull together, a time for the dying person to "tie up loose ends" and to say goodbye.

Teaching Strategies/Learning Opportunities

a. Open-Ended Sentences. Have students title the top of a piece of paper: "IF I KNEW I WAS DYING . . ." Then have them complete the following open-ended sentences:
(1) I would want my family to . . .
(2) I would want my friends to . . .
(3) I would want my doctor to . . .
(4) I would want to talk to . . .
On the back of the paper have students draw a picture symbolizing the rest of their life if they had one year left to live. Let students share their papers with others in the class. Responses may be listed on the board for discussion purposes.

b. Guest Speaker. Ask a counselor, a member of the clergy, or someone from the community with experience in dealing with the needs of the dying to talk to the class. The focus should be on the needs of the dying person and the way to talk to this peson and his/her family. (Show the speaker the content outline before coming to help organize the presentation.)
    After the speaker has left, have students write a short reaction to the presentation. Ask them to write what they liked and did not like about the

speaker, and if they recommend that the teacher invite this speaker again to another class. Share the general results of the evaluation with the class.

Evaluation Activity

Give students the following problem to work on:
You have just found out that your best friend's grandfather is dying. It seems that the illness will be long and drawn out. Your friend is very close to his/her grandfather and wants to make the most of the time they have left. Your friend knows that you have had a class on death and dying, and so he/she comes to you for advice. What will you tell your friend about the needs of his/her dying grandfather?

Collect the papers and evaluate the students' abilities to analyze the situation and to give helpful advice. Read aloud to the class a few outstanding examples of advice.

Resources

It is possible to list current resources related to death education, but materials are appearing regularly in the literature and in the marketplace. Journals such as *Death Education* and *Omega* can be helpful in keeping up-to-date on the issues, as well as providing reviews of pertinent new media resources and books. A categorical listing of materials appropriate for the classroom compiled by Steven Schwartz in 1977 provided a starting point for health educators in previewing materials for the classroom (6). A new listing of this sort should be made about every three years during the 1980's. Funeral directors in many communities are also becoming more concerned with their role as educator. Often they can be helpful resource people.

Further Considerations

Perhaps one of the most important questions for death education in the schools is Who will teach it? Crase and Crase warn that "some formal process must be instituted to ensure that those who teach are qualified and are capable of handling sensitive issues" (7). If the subject is to be integrated into health education, it must of course become a part of pre-service training for school health educators. This is the easy part. More difficult is the preparation of those health educators who are already teaching but who have not had any training in this area, as well as those who are designated to teach health but who have not been trained in health education and/or death education. This responsibility may devolve upon the professional organizations concerned with the quality of health education in the schools whose involvement could be two-pronged: (1) to provide a national stance that training in this area is necessary, and (2) to facilitate a model for training seminars and to publish the details on implementation of such seminars in professional journals. Alliance should be made between organizations concerned with health education, such as the Association for the Advancement of Health Education (AAHE), the American School Health Association (ASHA), and the School Health Section of the American Public Health Association (APHA); and organizations concerned with death education, such as the Forum for Death Education and Counseling, Inc. (8), and the Foundation of Thanatology (9).

In 1977, Goldsmith found that pre-service health educators looking forward to a teaching career felt comfortable or quite comfortable in teaching youngsters about death and dying (10). The next year Steinhausen explored what students really perceived as ideal death education (11). Though there was a slight preference for a course with much personal interaction with values and perceptions on death (particularly among females and those with a fairly recent death experience), when asked to design an ideal course, respondents recommended about equal parts of the following: (1) factual lecture presentations; (2) activities such as field trips to a funeral home and to the intensive care unit in a hospital, panel discussions, and thought-provoking films; and (3) confrontational activities such as "What would you do if you had only a week to live?" "Write your own epitaph . . .," and emotion-stirring films. He suggested that teachers inform students in advance of the "balance" their unit on death will have so that maximum benefit can accrue. Additional investigations similar to these will be necessary in order to chart a proper direction for death education in the future.

In conclusion, then, between 1980 and 1989 death education will become a natural and noncontroversial part of health education if (1) there is careful and humanistic planning to integrate it into health education where it fits appropriately, and (2) provisions are made for training so that teachers are helped to deal with this particularly sensitive area. When these goals are achieved, we shall be closer to the overall goal of education about death: to enhance and give meaning to *life*.

REFERENCES

1. Russell, Robert D., and Purdy, Candace O. *Coping with Death and Dying.* Glenview, Ill.: Scott, Foresman and Co., 1980. 64 pp. (With *Teacher's Guide,* 15 pp.)

2. Sliepcevich, Elena M. "Curriculum Development: A Macroscopic or Microscopic View?" *National Elementary Principal* 48 (November 1968): 16.

3. Hoyman, Howard S. "New Frontiers in Health." *Journal of School Health* 43 (September 1973): 423.

4. School Health Education Study. *Health Education: A Conceptual Approach.* Washington, D.C.: School Health Education Study, 1967.

5. Middleton, Kathleen Hoyt. "A Conceptual Approach to Death and Dying Education." Master's thesis, California State University, Long Beach, 1977.

6. Schwartz, Steven. "Death Education: Suggested Readings and Audiovisuals." *Journal of School Health* 47 (December 1977): 607–09.

7. Crase, Darrel, and Crase, Dixie R. "Emerging Dimensions of Death Education." *Health Education* (January/February 1979): 28.

8. Forum for Death Education and Counseling, Inc., P.O. Box 1226, Arlington, Va. 22210.

9. Foundation of Thanatology, 630 West 168th St., New York, N.Y. 10021.

10. Goldsmith, Malcolm D. "Future Health Educators and Death Education." Ph.D. dissertation, Southern Illinois University, Carbondale, 1978.

11. Steinhausen, Glenn W. "Identification of Variables Which Predict College Students' Acceptance of Described Teaching Approaches for Courses in Death Education." Ph.D. dissertation, Southern Illinois University, Carbondale, 1979.

CHAPTER 12

Internationalizing Health Education
Marian V. Hamburg

Predicting the future is always risky. Even when all reasonable indicators point in a clear direction, unexpected events can radically change the course. Forecasts of developments on a global scale are particularly difficult because of their susceptibility to the vagaries of political and economic developments in various parts of the world. Therefore they are probably even less reliable than prognostications of a local nature. Nevertheless, the current increase of activities related to international health appears to be a continuing trend in which health education will fully participate. The political stresses affecting relationships between countries may change the geographical areas of interest, but the internationalizing of health education will surely continue. There has been too much progress to turn back.

DEVELOPMENTS IN INTERNATIONAL HEALTH

Interest in international health expanded greatly during the 70's. The programs of the United Nations and its specialized agencies, including not only the World Health Organization and its regional offices, but also the World Bank, the United Nations Development Program, and the United Nations Children's Fund, were largely responsible for highlighting international health needs, especially those of developing countries.

The scale of international health involvement of the United States government also grew significantly during this period. The Department of Health, Education, and Welfare was engaged in a broad spectrum of activities outside the country, as well as in domestic activities directly related to the health of other countries. The Office of Education's Division of International Education, through the Fulbright-Hayes Training Grants, supported faculty research, doctoral dissertations, and curriculum development projects abroad, some of them specific to health education.

The increased attention to world health concerns also spread to professional organizations. The 70's saw the addition of a new section on International Health in the American Public Health Association, a new standing committee on International Health Education in the American School Health Association, and the organization of a viable North American Regional Office of the International Union for Health Education. The National Council on International Health expanded its organizational members. And the International Health Resources Consortium was established, with business and industry sponsorship.

In addition, the Tenth International Conference on Health Education was held (in London, in 1979), as were a number of other international health meetings, most of which were devoted to specific topics such as smoking, alcoholism, voluntary sterilization, and primary health care.

The 70's also brought more internationalism to elementary and secondary schools. There was a new curriculum emphasis on culture, with the utilization of local resources of an ethnic nature for teaching and learning. As people traveled more, it was natural to want to learn more about what was being experienced outside the United States.

Colleges and universities also become more internationalized, both by accident and design. A major reason was the continuing increase in the number of foreign students coming from many countries, some of which were nonexistent at the beginning of the decade. The very presence of these students on our college campuses provided a natural resource for learning about diverse cultures.

New academic programs flourished with federal funding for foreign language and foreign area study centers. In the field of health education, courses with an international flavor appeared. Under a variety of titles—International Health, World Health Problems, Issues in International Health, Nutrition Around the World, Cultural Attitudes Toward Human Sexuality, and World Population—many health education departments began to offer pre-service health educators multicultural learning experiences.

Study Abroad

The most interesting of the international developments in universities are the programs for study abroad. The concept is not new, but it has been applied only recently to health education. Of the several approaches to the study of world health, internationalizing the context in which learning takes place is by far the most relevant. There is simply no substitute for being "on location" to understand the social, cultural, political, and economic conditions affecting health. The active emotional experiences of daily living in another culture provide insights not possible through remote, passive, academic study. The authenticity and dynamism of the learning environment cannot be reproduced by textbooks, case studies, or even the best of the media. A country visited, especially if the visit is long enough and the cultural involvement deep enough, is never again "foreign." Its people are never again strange—only different. They are no longer impersonal populations, but real personalities who love, hate, relate to families, struggle for food, recognition, and self-fulfillment—and who work, sleep, and eat much as we do.

Although the critical factor in intercultural learning is "being there," there is a qualitative aspect. If "being there" means staying in some hostelry in protected luxury while discussing the problems of population, hunger, environmental threats, and primary health care through statistical presentations by health experts and education specialists, then the subsequent learnings may have little relationship to the compelling problems of the people outside the hotel. Some international seminars and conferences in such settings have become part of a thriving growth industry, sponsored for profit and pleasure by shrewd, clever entrepreneurs who can guarantee to keep participants at an antiseptic distance from the real problems, while providing an atmosphere for theoretical prescriptions and solutions.

The living arrangements for participants in study abroad programs make an important contribution to intercultural learning. Staying in homes with local families or in student residences with native students is far more desirable than establishing isolated "little Americas."

Purposes. Specific objectives of overseas health programs vary, but the general goals are similar. They provide opportunities for examining health problems as they present themselves in another culture, and for comparing approaches to their solutions. They help develop understanding, skills, and attitudes appropriate to health education in international or intercultural settings, including, almost paradoxically, the "back home situations." And they promote an awareness of the inter-relatedness of health and social and economic development.

Programs may deal generally with health education or may relate specifically to nutrition, health care systems, addictions, rural health, family planning, or other current concern. The focus of the program is closely interrelated with the choice of location, the leadership, the participants, and the nature of the activities.

Program patterns afford considerable variety. The amount of time spent abroad, for instance, may range from a week to a year or more. Many programs, especially those for graduate students, are planned for summer or winter vacation periods. Typically, these are seminars or courses involving faculty leadership from the home institution, in collaboration with health and education professionals from the country visited. They usually employ a range of teaching methods, including lecture, discussion, observation, field work, reading, research, and the use of the media.

Internships, which provide students with supervised work experience abroad, are a growing trend, especially in universities offering a degree program in international health.

Activities. The distinguishing feature of study abroad programs is the utilization of the resources of the country visited: *their* institutions, *their* teachers and health professionals, *their* communities, and *their* materials to learn about *their* health programs.

A group studying sex education in Sweden, for instance, may profitably spend an entire day in the curriculum materials center of the local board of education, viewing and discussing films and other visual aids used in schools, with Swedish teachers on hand to interpret and explain.

In Kenya, a group may learn about health care through a series of visits which may include a sophisticated general hospital, a specialized hospital for leprosy, a primitive local health center, and the slum "office" of a traditional medical practitioner. The feelings experienced in watching treatment of a mental patient utilizing chanting, fire, water, and touching by the traditional doctor cannot be forgotten. The feelings experienced in watching lepers learn to carry out the daily chores of living in ways that avoid further loss of their fingers and toes are also unforgettable. There is no question about the heightened impact of educational experiences that are *felt* as well as intellectualized. When they are also viewed more objectively than is possible in one's own culture, the resulting learning can be related more easily to the home setting.

Examples of practical experiences that may be a part of overseas study include working side by side with a British health educator in conducting smoking cessation sessions, or providing in-service alcohol education to teachers, or conducting a house-to-house survey of attitudes toward family planning. Taking photographs, recording sounds, and collecting artifacts for use in teaching units at home are other appropriate activities for teachers at all levels. Overseas group projects for curriculum development, the counterpart of the familiar curriculum development workshops in the United States, are excellent for ensuring an acceptable means of extending the experience, at least partially, to other students.

FUTURE PROJECTIONS

Looking ahead, it is logical to expect international programs not only to expand, but to emphasize even more study abroad. The most effective programs will be of sufficient duration and depth to provide much more than tourist impressions. Experience has shown that a single location for a longer period is definitely preferable to several locations for short periods.

Group leadership may be expected to improve as more of the regular faculty and staff of sponsoring institutions gain experience in planning and directing programs. Study abroad will be integrated with broader programs of study or a curriculum leading toward a degree. Because regular faculty members will accompany groups on a continuing basis, they will be better able to prepare participants for the experience through prior orientation designed to reduce the cultural shock. Opportunity for debriefing or summing up the meaning of the experience will also be built into the program. Reunions of group members are not only joyous occasions, but are reenforcers of the learning, as well as opportunities to make critical analyses.

Standards for selection of students going abroad may be expected to be even higher than for campus study. In addition to the usual grade point averages, motivations for study, and past professional experiences, an important criterion to be considered will be adaptability to unfamiliar environments.

The strengthening of linkages between institutions in the United States and overseas will facilitate collaboration on a continuing basis. This is an important factor to the success of any program, since it is the overseas collaborators who make many arrangements, identify local resources, and also serve as the interpreters of the culture. Ideally there should be reverse study abroad for the overseas collaborators of foreign groups hosted by U.S. institutions. In a practical sense, this is difficult to arrange because of costs. Students from the United States are accustomed to paying their own way, but students from other countries generally are not. Until financing is available, these programs will continue, for the most part, to be one-way.

Knowledge of a country's language is of critical importance. Without such skills, there can be only partial communication, which results in limited understanding of what is observed. Many institutions have restricted their programs to English-speaking countries such as Jamaica, Barbados, or the United Kingdom, or to countries where English is widely known and used, as it is in Sweden, Denmark, and Japan. The future direction should be toward language as well as health study. Even brief study of language "on the spot" helps understanding enormously. Ideally, participants should be bilingual.

Program evaluation, probably the most difficult aspect of study abroad, will require more attention. While gains in knowledge are easy to assess, shifts in participant attitudes toward other people and nations are more difficult. Because of the interrelatedness of health problems from one culture to another, one expected outcome of these study programs is attitude change favoring more open international relations generally and greater intercultural cooperation in health matters specifically. It is important to ascertain whether such change is actually taking place. Insufficient literature on the subject is available.

Although the emphasis of this chapter has been on the study aspects of international travel, it cannot be overlooked that such programs are attractive, interesting, and valuable to leaders and participants alike. That very factor contributes to their growth. The experiences are stimulating and challenging, and may lead to new jobs, although it should be noted that employment opportunities for U.S. citizens in other countries are limited. However, a firsthand knowledge of another country can often enhance the ability to work with people from the many cultures in our own country. Overall, the health field is expanding. Job opportunities for health educators with international experience, intercultural understanding, and the ability to speak more than one language are bright.

The main factors that may curb the growth of study abroad are economic and political. At the end of the 70's the cost of programs, in terms of transportation, food, and housing, was still reasonable in many parts of the world. Countries where living costs are high will be less often selected as study sites. For example, there may be more programs in Mexico and fewer in Japan.

Political conditions must also be considered. How friendly are a country's relationships with the United States? How safe are visitors to the country? How welcome? Changes in governments will continue to influence site selection.

Despite obstacles, however, the internationalization of health education will surely continue. It is an important part of the future of the profession.

CHAPTER 13

Teaching Values in Health Education
Gus T. Dalis and Ben B. Strasser

Mr. Russell: It's about time we've started to teach values in our health education classes. It's taken only seventy years.

Mr. Winkelman: I hear what you're saying, but that's not exactly true. Values are there every time we make a decision about what to teach.

Mr. Russell: Sure, but we're talking now about teaching kids values in the classroom. We haven't been teaching them health-related values as a goal in our teaching. That's what I mean.

Ms. Nolte: Right. I'm glad we're finally beginning to do more about teaching values, too. But, what about everything else we've been doing? Does bringing values into health education mean that we drop all that we're doing, or should values just be added as another goal? Teaching values *alone* certainly can't be all there is to a comprehensive program in health education.

What about these statements? Is it true that values have not been included in the health education curriculum for seventy years as suggested by Mr. Russell? Many would disagree that the addition of values to our goals for health education is recent. Many health education historical buffs would support Mr. Winkelman's position, that from the time the subject was first taught, values have influenced professional decisionmaking about what we teach and how we teach it. Their position is that the influence of values was therefore *indirect*.

116

This chapter briefly traces the emerging role of values in health education, from a foundation for curriculum decisions to a part of that curriculum itself; it then develops the major purpose: to suggest some ways to deal with values, more directly and more systematically, in the health education curriculum of the 80's and beyond. One word of caution, however, before you read on. Because this chapter is about values in health education, our comments are directed to that topic. For the record, though, we agree with Ms. Nolte. Teaching health values is not all there is or should be in a health education curriculum.

VALUES AND THE EVOLUTION OF HEALTH EDUCATION

The history of school health education recounts the attempts of educators to influence the behavior of their students, in the best interests of those students. To present this brief review, we have organized our comments according to the following eras: ca. 1900—Anatomy/ Physiology; ca. 1920—Health Habits; ca. 1940—Health Knowledge; ca. 1960—Health Concepts; and ca. 1970—Health Values Clarification/ Awareness (1). It should be pointed out that the eras are identified as generally characterizing national trends. There have been and are, of course, many local exceptions to these generalities.

The first direct health education in this century consisted of a series of health lessons, teaching students about the anatomy and physiology of the human body. The hope was that as students learned about the structure and function of the body, they would value it and take care of it, behaving healthfully. Because this approach did not achieve the results expected, the next era emphasized health habits directly as *rules for health.* The rules were presented and frequently recited. Gold stars were awarded for rules followed, and students played health rule games. Values were not taught directly, but underlying the rules were such values as cleanliness, proper nutrition, and clean, noncarious teeth. Reciting rules did not necessarily translate into actual health behaviors, however.

Educators considered the reasons for this and concluded that students didn't understand *why* these health habits were important. Thus began the era of health knowledge. Still emphasizing health habits, the curriculum was based on the interests and needs of children and youth, as well as on societal health problems, but it had a strong knowledge base. Despite this goal of having students deal with health problems rationally and reasonably, curriculum guides also introduced values for the first time—in the form of health *attitudes.* Because most teachers seemed to feel more comfortable with the factual content, however, attitudes were more evident in the curriculum goal statements than in the classroom.

The 1960's will be remembered as the era of the "knowledge explosion." The body of knowledge for a good health course could no longer consist of material the teacher remembered from college classes. With the prospect of an indefinite continuation of increased information and data, curriculum writers began the era of concepts—generalizations and "big ideas" as *organizers* for all information students might encounter. Although the attitudes and behaviors of the previous era were retained as learning goals, they were now more often referred to as the *affective* and *action* domains of the concepts.

Hence, teaching toward values was becoming more accepted among health educators, but not yet a part of most daily classroom instruction. The major concern was to influence students so that they would initiate behavior to foster high-level wellness. As the 60's developed, however, there was ample evidence that problems such as drug and alcohol abuse, poor eating and exercise habits, and smoking were increasing rather than decreasing. Concepts were not a magic answer. Therefore Values Clarification, conceptualized by Sidney Simon, was incorporated into health teaching through various activities (2, 3, 4, 5).

A second approach, Values Awareness, developed by Dalis and Strasser (6), intended to help students (1) become aware of their own values and the values of their peers, and (2) learn to explicate their own values. This approach rests on either a discussion or activity format in which students make value judgments or report courses of action they feel are appropriate to the topic or situation under consideration. As students participate in the discussion format, the teacher uses specific teaching behaviors to encourage students to move beyond the expression of value judgments and courses of action to the values that *underlie* these value judgments and/or courses of action. In the activity format certain steps in the activity itself lead students to the recognition of underlying values that they or their classmates may have, relative to a particular health topic or situation (7). Not every group or individual activity lends itself to values awareness, however. A simple way to determine this is to note if students discuss their values per se during the activity, or to conduct a post-activity evaluation, and invite students to state their values about the activity topic or situation. If, after participating in such an activity, they are unable to report their values, then the activity is probably not useful in facilitating values awareness.

Approaches such as Values Clarification and Values Awareness became important in health education because of the belief that if individuals are to be more effective health decisionmakers, they must have a knowledge of their own health values. Because of the tremendous popularity of these approaches among many health educators and their overwhelming acceptance by students, however, some health education curricula dropped or severely minimized an equally critical emphasis on health data, information, generalizations, and concepts. In some school districts health education itself became only Values Clarification, as if to deny that rational decisionmaking is founded on data and ideas as well as on values.

HEALTH EDUCATION IN THE 80'S AND BEYOND

Unquestionably, modern-day health education programs have as their primary goal the sharpening of the student's ability to make more rational health decisions. Rational decisionmaking requires the consideration of both relevant information or data *and* one's values. An emphasis on decisionmaking is therefore the best justification for teaching data, information, generalizations, and concepts (the necessary knowledge), and for helping students become aware of their values. But, while helping students become aware of their values is important, instruction in this area should go beyond the goals of awareness alone. In addition, health educators should also feel the responsibility to motivate the development of the student's health-related values, rather than leave this development to chance. This is called Values Development by Design.

Teaching toward values development begins with the identification of specific values to be taught. Some health-related values might include cleanliness, disease prevention, balanced diet, responsible sexual behavior, appropriate sleep, physical conditioning, accident prevention, responsible social health behavior, responsibility for one's own health, being well informed about health-related issues and problems, and so on. No doubt, it would be possible to identify many more health-related values. The task of identifying the health values to be taught is not an easy one. But it is necessary if comprehensive values development by design is to take place in the health classroom.

The first step in preparing to teach for values development is to select the health value to be taught. The next step is to identify or create an event or situation that centers on the value in action. Examples may be found in a story, film, newspaper or magazine article, role-playing situation, case study, dramatization, or simulation. In the situation or event, the behavior of one or more people, either consistent or inconsistent with the value being taught, is presented. Consistent behavior should yield positive consequences to the individual, while inconsistent behavior should yield negative consequences.

Once the event or situation has been selected, the act of teaching first includes any instruction necessary to familiarize students with both the value being studied and the behaviors that are consistent and inconsistent with the value. Then, students use the material or are involved in an activity intended to emphasize the value, the behavior, and its consequences. In other words, they learn to recognize the positive consequences that may result from living consistent with a value and the negative consequences that may result from living inconsistent with that value. Finally, the teacher summarizes the lesson by relating the value, the behaviors, and the consequences as a way of affirming the relationship among the three factors.

To illustrate the flow of a typical values development lesson, consider the following example:

SELECT VALUE	Using the school curriculum guide, the high school health teacher selects the value *Responsible Social Health Behavior*.
SELECT, IDENTIFY, OR ADAPT AVAILABLE MATERIALS OR CREATE A SUITABLE ACTIVITY	The teacher locates a case study in supplementary health materials. This case study recounts the story of a girl who, while going steady with one boy, contracts gonorrhea from someone else. She is afraid to tell her steady boyfriend, with whom she has occasional sexual relations. Shortly thereafter, her boyfriend also contracts the disease.
INTRODUCE VALUE	The lesson begins as the teacher informs students that they will be working on the value, *Responsible Social Health Behavior*. To do so, they will be reading and discussing a case study about a girl whose behavior is inconsistent with this value, in order to learn about the effect of her behavior on herself and others.
CONSIDER VALUE-RELATED BEHAVIORS	Next, to review the meaning of *Responsible Social Health Behavior*, the teacher invites students to recount some specific behavioral examples of this value. As they do so, the teacher lists their comments on the board under the heading Value: *Responsible Social Health Behavior*. Students make statements such as the following: 1. Using a tissue when you sneeze 2. Avoiding crowds when you have a contagious illness 3. Bathing daily 4. . . .

120

CONSIDER VALUE-RELATED BEHAVIOR CONSEQUENCES	After listing five or six such behaviors on the chalkboard, the teacher solicits comments from students about (1) positive consequences when behaviors consistent with the value are implemented and (2) possible negative consequences when those behaviors are ignored.
ACTIVITY INTRODUCE ACTIVITY READ JUDGE BEHAVIOR	Next, the teacher introduces the case study students are to read. They are given five minutes to read through the story. After the reading time has concluded, students are organized in small groups whose task is first to decide whether the behavior of the girl was consistent or inconsistent with the value *Responsible Social Health Behavior.* Then they are to report the bases for their judgment—what the girl did or didn't do but should have done.
CITE ILLUSTRATION BEHAVIORS	Following these small group discussions, each group reports. At the same time, the teacher or a student records whether the girl's behavior was consistent or inconsistent with the value, and what the girl did or should have done.
REPORT CONSEQUENCES OF VALUE-RELATED BEHAVIOR	Next, the total class reviews the girl's behavior that was inconsistent with the value as listed on the chalkboard and reports consequences (negative in this instance) for the girl or others involved. The teacher also invites group members to report what they think the girl should have done if she were to behave consistent with the value *Responsible Social Health Behavior.*
	During this discussion the teacher reaffirms the relationship between the value, the behaviors, and the consequences.

SOME FINAL COMMENTS

This approach in teaching for values development by design is not necessarily new or complicated. Many would agree, however, that such an approach has been missing in health education and is now desperately needed in order to help students develop specified health-related values. The great difficulty in teaching toward values development is to avoid the tendency to become dogmatic or manipulative. The more objective the teacher is, the more effective he or she will be in achieving the goal of facilitating the development of these values in students.

One dilemma in teaching toward values development is the identification of values that are generally accepted by a community. As long as the teacher is successful in selecting values with which the community agrees, then the instruction in values development is called *good* teaching. If, however, the teacher inadvertently identifies and teaches toward a value, such as *responsible sexual behavior,* about which the community may not be in agreement, this teaching may be labeled *brainwashing* and may in turn lead to disciplinary action by the school board. The best protection for the health educator interested in implanting values development in the classroom is therefore to restrict such lessons to values specified or outlined in the district health curriculum.

A word of caution to panacea seekers: There is no easy way to attain the highly complex goals identified for health education. History affirms this fact. Rational health-related decisionmaking requires data, information, generalizations, concepts, and values. In recommending the inclusion of values development by design in the curriculum, we are not suggesting that it supplant the teaching of anatomy and physiology, health habits, health knowledge, health concepts, and health-related values clarification/awareness. Indeed, at present these approaches, together with values development by design, seem to be the elements that must be skillfully balanced in the curriculum for holistic health education in the 80's. The challenge to the health educator is to devise and implement a curriculum reflecting each of these orientations in a proper perspective and dealing with them at a level of complexity appropriate for her/his students.

REFERENCES

1. Means, Richard K. *Historical Perspectives on School Health.* Thorofare, N.J.: Charles B. Slack, 1975.

2. Simon, Sidney B.; Howe, Leland W.; and Kirschenbaum, Howard. *Values Clarification: A Handbook of Practical Strategies for Teachers and Students.* New York: Hart Publishing Co., 1972.

3. Harmin, Merrill; Kirschenbaum, Howard; and Simon, Sidney B. *Clarifying Values Through Subject Matter.* Minneapolis: Winston Press, 1973.

4. Read, Donald A.; Simon, Sidney B.; and Goodman, Joel B. *Health Education: The Search for Values.* Englewood Cliffs, N.J.: Prentice-Hall, 1977.

5. Read, Donald A. *Looking In: Exploring One's Personal Health Values.* Englewood Cliffs, N.J.: Prentice-Hall, 1977.

6. Loggins, Dennis. "Clarifying What and How Well?" *Health Education* (March/April 1976): 2–5.

7. Dalis, Gus T., and Strasser, Ben B. *Teaching Strategies for Values Awareness and Decision Making in Health Education.* Thorofare, N.J.: Charles B. Slack, 1977.

8. California State Department of Education. *Curriculum Guide for Nutrition Education Preschool Age Through Grade Six.* Sacramento, Calif.: California Nutrition Education and Training Program, 1979. (Draft Copy)

Afterword

Robert D. Russell

What has been said about the field of health education for the future? There is considerable prognosis that it should be more positive and more holistic. There should be more emphasis on eating well, exercising, relating positively with others—not only to prevent problems, but to promote positive health. We need to achieve a better balance between body and mind, and to increase the capacity of the body to be positively adaptive to stresses that will undoubtedly be part of life in the United States in future years.

There is a call for education about sexuality to be more holistic, and for healing to be more holistic, involving the spirit as well as the body and the mind. Alcohol education should encourage perception of the values in both drinking and not drinking, and drug education should stress a more positive approach to life. One of the newer entrants into the curriculum, death education, is important not only because it can help solve the problem of facing death, but because it can help encourage a more positive sense of life—an appreciation of the importance of living each day as fully and joyfully as possible.

This little volume has dealt not only with subjects or topic areas, but with approaches to education about health. Again, approaches should be more positive, but also, as Jose admonishes, less sexist. We should not assign roles to people because of sex unless the individual

123

desires such a role. In other words, traditional sex roles are fine, but only as individuals agree to assume them for their positive values.

Attempts should be made to extend health education to other countries and cultures and to encourage an openness to other views of life and other approaches to health and healing. Dalis and Strasser advocate going beyond values awareness and clarification to values development by design in any subject areas that cannot be adequately taught without some consideration of conflicting values.

In addition, there are problems to which health education must address itself—heart disease, cancer, drug abuse, alcohol abuse, smoking, premarital pregnancies, venereal diseases, advertising, quackery—the list could go on. Learners need to know what these problems are, how to prevent or alleviate them, should they "appear." Health education has always had some crisis orientation, which will continue. But problem orientation should be only a part, not the essence, of this teaching/learning area.

In relation to both ageism and scientific medicine, an interesting value question arises. In our general Western way of thinking it is difficult to value two things that seem to conflict or compete with each other. During the next decade can we come to esteem being old and not so vigorous without diminishing our value of youth and vigor? Can we appreciate a wider variety of approaches to health and healing without losing the value of scientific medical approaches?

As suggested earlier, when health education is in the school curriculum, it is usually there in response to a real or perceived crisis. We professionals must continue to work so that it may achieve a more positive base. Algebra is taught because of the perception that such learning is important, not because society has some problem that will worsen without algebraic knowledge. Health education needs more of this rationale.

Health is a means to higher-quality functioning in all the dimensions of living—mental, spiritual, social, emotional, and physical. Health *is* the quality of the individual's functioning in the total environment. Health is *also* the quality of the total environment in which individuals have to function. In addition, health is the capacity to adapt appropriately and creatively to life's situations. Girdano provides the last words—with advice to worry less about the future, live a richer today, love more and hurry less, "for your destination is within you and in constant, easy reach."

Stephen J. Bender is Professor and Chair of Health Science at San Diego State University. He is the author of four health science texts and numerous periodical articles, many of which deal with human sexuality. His extracurricular interests are jogging, cycling, real estate, plants, antiques, and sports cars.

Charles R. Carroll is Professor of Physiology and Health Science at Ball State University. He is co-author of *Health, Quackery, and the Consumer,* a consumer health text; and of *Health: The Science of Human Adaptation,* a general health text for college students.

Gus. T. Dalis is Consultant in Health Education and Co-Chair of the Teaching Strategies Center for the Los Angeles County Schools. One of the authors of the School Health Education Study, he is co-author of *Health Instruction: Theory and Application* and *Teaching Strategies for Values Awareness and Decision-Making in Health Education.* He develops and conducts training sessions for teachers on values awareness and teaching strategies.

Marigold A. Edwards is Associate Professor of Health and Physical Education at the University of Pittsburgh. A New Zealander, she came to this country in 1964 for graduate work. Her professional expertise and published papers are in the areas of racket sports and fitness, weight control, and stress management.

Daniel A. Girdano is Co-Executive Director and one of the Senior Faculty at the Ecotopia Clinical Training and Research Institute in Winter Park, Colorado. He is the author of several books, including *The Holistic Approach to Controlling Stress and Tension* and *Come Play with Me, I'm Yours.* His pioneering holistic approach is becoming widely used in education, industry, and individual counseling.

Marion V. Hamburg is Professor and Chairperson of the Department of Health Education, and head of the graduate degree program in International Health Education at New York University. As the result of an international component which she initiated at NYU in 1974, all graduate students are now encouraged to take at least one seminar in the cultural setting of another country.

Nancy Lee Jose is Assistant Professor of Health and Phsyical Education at the University of Kentucky. Her major research has been in perceptions of aging by women of different ages.

Kathleen Hoyt Middleton is the Director of Curriculum for the School Health Education Project, a part of the National Center for Health Education. A former junior high school teacher, she is the author of *A Conceptual Approach to Death and Dying Education,* a complete curriculum for junior high.

Adogbeji Lucky Oghojafor is a Nigerian, with degrees in journalism, rehabilitation, and health education. He is currently working in an agency in California, awaiting assignment within the World Health Organization. A paraplegic, he desires to encourage the coming together of scientifically trained medical people and native, traditional healers, in order that each may learn from the other.

Geraldine Rockett is Associate Director of the Counseling Center at Dickinson College, Carlisle, Pennsylvania. Her professional interests are in personal/emotional, career, and health/wellness counseling. Her experience has been with mental health centers and outreach programs.

Robert D. Russell is Professor of Health Education at Southern Illinois University at Carbondale. He is the author of NEA/AMA's *Health Education,* of *The Last Bell Is Ringing,* and a co-author of *Coping with Death and Dying.* A leader in the movement for positive, holistic health education, he has received honor awards from Eta Sigma Gamma and the American School Health Association.

Warren E. Schaller is Professor and Chair of the Department of Physiology and Health Science at Ball State University. He authored *The School Health Program* and co-authored *Health, Quackery, and the Consumer.* He is past president of the American School Health Association, and national president of Eta Sigma Gamma, the national health science honorary society.

Ben B. Strasser is Consultant and Co-Chair of the Teaching Strategies Center for the Los Angeles County Schools. A former public school science teacher, he is the senior author of *Teaching Toward Inquiry* and a co-author of *Teaching Strategies for Values Awareness and Decision-Making in Health Education.*

Betty W. Tevis is Chief of the Section on Heart Health Education in the Young of the American Heart Association. A former public school teacher and university professor, she coordinates the development of heart health education programs for youth, working with AHA affiliates and school systems throughout the United States.